Algernon Taylor

Convent life in Italy

Algernon Taylor

Convent life in Italy

ISBN/EAN: 9783741199172

Manufactured in Europe, USA, Canada, Australia, Japa

Cover: Foto ©Andreas Hilbeck / pixelio.de

Manufactured and distributed by brebook publishing software (www.brebook.com)

Algernon Taylor

Convent life in Italy

CONVENT LIFE
IN
ITALY

CONVENT LIFE

IN

ITALY

BY

ALGERNON TAYLOR.

LONDON:
CHARLES J. SKEET, KING WILLIAM STREET,
CHARING CROSS.
MDCCCLXII.

LONDON:
A. Schulze, Printer, 13, Poland Street.

[The right of translation is reserved.]

PREFACE.

THIS volume is compiled from the writer's Journal of several tours in Italy, made between the years 1856 and 1859. Having had, although a protestant, the advantage accidentally thrown in his path of an introduction to the Superior of a Convent at Genoa, where he remained some weeks on a visit, this led, indirectly, to introductions to other monasteries in different parts of Italy, in which he successively became a visitor. The author has ventured, in the following pages, to publish the result of his experience and observation in these several monasteries, believing the subject (however inadequately handled) to be both interesting in itself, and one which has not hitherto been treated in books of Italian travel, the peculiar opportunities enjoyed by the author having probably never been accorded to any previous traveller.

That the monastic type of Christian perfection differs widely from the ideas of Christianity prevailing in protestant countries—and that Monasticism, and the Church of Rome generally, are for the most part ranged among the opponents of free thought and liberal institutions—are no reasons why the English public should not make itself acquainted with facts illustrating the actual working of the monastic system at the present day. This volume is essentially a narrative of facts, the author having abstained from entering into any controversial questions, whether of religion or politics, contenting himself with an impartial narration of facts that have fallen under his personal observation, and which are not easy of access. The philosophical inquirer will accept the facts, even though he may dissent from the philosophy on which the monastic system is based, or condemn the political results to which it appears to conduce.

Recent political events in Italy, moreover, may be expected to impart something of an historical character to these notes on Italian monasteries; for, owing to the suppression of many of the religious houses of Italy—and among them, it is to be presumed, some, at least, of those noticed in the present volume—the description of these here given may possibly constitute a record of their appearance, and of the manner of life led within their walls, during the last days of their monastic existence.

The author desires to add that he did not entertain the idea of publishing any part of his Journal, until after his return from the Italian tours here described. This circumstance, while it tends to free the narrative from the evils incident to mere book-making, has at the same time necessarily led to the omission of some details, which, with more copious memoranda, might have been supplied.

CONTENTS.

CHAPTER I.

Convent of San Bartolommeo degli Armeni . . . 1

CHAPTER II.

Genoa and its Convents continued—Journey to Rome 29

CHAPTER III.

Holy Week at Rome 52

CHAPTER IV.

The Churches of Rome 77

CHAPTER V.

Monastic Life at Rome 95

CHAPTER VI.

State of Clerical Education and Monastic Discipline in Italy 130

CHAPTER VII.

Convents of Rome continued 141

CHAPTER VIII.

Pedestrian Excursion to Rural Convents . . 156

CHAPTER IX.

Festival of Corpus Christi—Audience of the Pope—Return to England 183

CHAPTER X.

Convent of San Barnaba 197

CHAPTER XI.

Carnival at Genoa—Visits to Religious Houses at and near Genoa 226

CHAPTER XII.

Excursion to the Convent of Campi . . . 239

CHAPTER XIII.

Pedestrian Tour to Convents on the Riviera . 254

CHAPTER XIV.

The Certosa of Pavia 271

CHAPTER XV.

The Cathedral of Milan, and sundry Monasteries in Northern Italy 283

CHAPTER XVI.

Convents at Naples 303

CHAPTER XVII.

Miscellaneous Memoranda concerning Italian Monasteries 318

APPENDIX I.—Lord Macaulay and Laurence Sterne on Begging Friars 335

APPENDIX II.—List of Italian Monasteries visited by the Author 341

Notes 344

CONVENT LIFE
IN
ITALY.

CHAPTER I.

Convent of San Bartolommeo degli Armeni.

IN the outskirts of Genoa, on a hill behind the town, stands the small Convent of San Bartolommeo degli Armeni. The district in which it is situated, as well as a neighbouring gate into Genoa, derive their name of San Bartolommeo from this ancient convent. Between five and six hundred years ago, a monastery was founded on this spot by some Armenian monks of the Order of St. Basil, who continued to dwell there until the suppression of their Order by the Papal See in 1656, when it passed into the hands of the Congregation of Regular Clerks of St. Paul, commonly called Barnabites, from a church of St. Barnabas at Milan, where the first house of the Order was founded in the sixteenth century. To this day, the convent is known by the name of San Bartolommeo degli Armeni, although since the year 1656 it has belonged to the Barnabites; and, besides its name, this convent retains several other reminiscences of the Armenian monks, such as a bust of St. Basil the Great (one of the patriarchs of Oriental monachism), over the convent gate, with an ancient inscription beneath; and in a niche at the top of the principal staircase is a full-length, though a very roughly executed, statue of the same Saint. There are, moreover, masses still celebrated in the convent church, for the souls of persons who died during the tenancy of the Armenians, and who left legacies to found chaplaincies for the performance of these masses.*

* The documents sometimes posted on the walls of sacristies in foreign churches, with the title of "Onera perpetua missarum," and containing a list of the

The Superior of San Bartolommeo was prevailed on through an excellent introduction with which I was provided, to receive me for a short time as a visitor to his convent. This was early in February, 1856. The present was the first occasion on which I had sojourned in a monastery, and many were the mediæval associations that arose in my mind as I followed the Superior up the broad stone staircase, and through the dimly lighted corridors which led to the room assigned to me. We passed through several large doors, each of which the Superior had to unlock to admit of our passage; and this unlocking and locking of ponderous doors in the gloom of night, and the most profound silence, added to the effect of the unusual but interesting circumstances in which I was thus placed. The room allotted to me opened into the main dormitory or corridor; and its windows, which looked on to the cloister

masses which the clergy of the particular church are bound to celebrate as trustees of funds bequeathed for this purpose, are curious, and often interesting from the length of time to which they go back.

and garden, commanded a fine view of Genoa and the Mediterranean. The chamber was paved with red brick, and its furniture consisted of a little bed in a recess, a table and chairs, an antiquated chest of drawers, a *prie-dieu*, a crucifix, and a few paintings and woodcuts representing religious subjects.

The external appearance of many, perhaps most, Italian monasteries of the richer or endowed orders, is very similar to that of an ordinary Italian house of large size, with a church adjoining it. The walls are usually of white or grey stone. The windows resemble those of a common house and are at about the same intervals, and protected from the rays of the sun by wooden blinds, painted green. As a general rule (although there are many exceptions to it, especially in the case of the larger abbeys and priories), it is only when you enter the building, and see the cloisters, the dormitories, the cells and the refectory, that you realize the fact that the great square edifice of white stone which you saw from without, is a monastery. San Bartolommeo degli

Armeni corresponds very much to this desscription. The convents of the poorer, or mendicant orders, on the other hand, are very different; for the long rows of tiny windows, placed in close proximity to one another (owing to the small dimensions of the cells of the friars) give them a marked character of their own. These Friaries present the appearance, for the most part, of long and rather low buildings of greyish stone, with two or three rows of diminutive windows, and roofs made of red tiles. The convent church stands generally by the side of the convent, immediately contiguous to the cloister, in the same way as our English Cathedrals are built, side by side with the adjoining cloister.

The Barnabites, to whom San Bartolommeo belongs, differ considerably from the mendicant orders, nor do they profess that extreme poverty which forms a marked characteristic of the Mendicant Friars. Like most of the Orders founded since the Reformation, in addition to the special duties of conventual life, they devote themselves to tuition, and the reader may judge of the services that they are acknowledged thus to render to the public, from the fact that the Barnabites are among the number of those excepted from the operation of the well-known law for the suppression of the monasteries in the kingdom of Sardinia, passed a few years ago. They do not profess any extraordinary rigidity of discipline, but live in a quiet, simple, regular manner, combining the retirement of monastic life with the more active duties of education. But although tuition is the general practice of the Barnabites, the particular convent of the Order of which I am speaking, San Bartolommeo, is an exception to the rule, for, on account of its being the novitiate of the province (where the novices pass their period of probation) no lay scholars are received there, so that the community lead a strictly retired and thoroughly monastic life.

As is usually the case with orders of men who perform active duties, whether teaching or otherwise, the Barnabites are exempted from the public celebration in choir of the Seven Canonical Hours of the Breviary, the daily recitation of which is obligatory on the Roman Catholic clergy of every denomination, and which in convents generally, are sung or said in choir by the assembled monks or nuns, as the case may be. This exemption, however, from the public recitation of the breviary, does not free them from the obligation of reading it privately, which attaches to every person in holy orders.*

The church of San Bartolommeo degli Armeni, externally, is plain in the extreme. It has, however, a quaint little belfry, whose oft-sounding bells are well known to those who have resided in that quarter of Genoa. The interior of the church contains several points of

* This ancient practice of the daily reading, by the clergy, of the seven parts of the breviary is regarded as a serious obligation in all Roman Catholic countries. It is founded on the 119th Psalm, "Seven times a day do I praise thee, because of thy righteous judgments." How much importance is attached, in practice, to this particular rule of clerical discipline by the clergy of Spain, for example, may be seen in Blanco White's 'Autobiography,' where he testifies to the strictness with which this regulation is there observed.

interest. These consist chiefly of a few paintings, including an ancient and highly curious one in the choir; an elegant white marble balustrade separating the chancel from the nave; and a chapel, in which is preserved a relic, esteemed of great value in Genoa, and called the "Santo Sudario." This, which is not to be confounded with the well-known "Santa Veronica," at Rome, is traditionally said to contain the impress of the Saviour's countenance, miraculously imparted to it. It is kept under a dozen locks, or thereabouts, the keys of which are in possession of various ecclesiastical and municipal personages, and whenever the relic is removed from the chapel (which happens only at Whitsuntide), a notarial deed is executed, certifying its restoration to the appointed place of security. It is recorded, that in the sixteenth century, this relic was carried off to Paris by two officers of Francis I., but that the king, at the earnest suit of the rightful owners, ordered it to be restored to them. It is to this circumstance that the extraordinary care that has since then been taken of the relic is attributed. Over the chapel of the 'Santo Sudario' are inscribed the words, Το αγιον μανδηλον.*

The cloister of this convent consists of little more than one side of a quadrangle, supported on ten handsome marble columns; and adjoining the cloister is the large "villa," or garden, belonging to the convent, planted mainly with vines trellised on high poles. The refectory at San Bartolommeo, like conventual refectories generally, is, in form, an oblong chamber, with the door at one end, and tables extending round the three other sides, the middle of the room being thus left free for the lay-brothers to bring in and remove the dishes. It contains several paintings, the principal of which, a Last Supper at the upper end, is attributed to Cambiaso, an old Genoese painter.

According to tradition, Cambiaso being on friendly terms with the Armenian monks, and happening to be the loser in some pastime in which a supper had been staked between them, satisfied the debt by presenting them with this

* The Holy Towel.

picture. Games of ball—especially with wooden balls of large size—form a frequent diversion of the religious orders in Italy, and were often indulged in, as a recreation, by the good fathers of San Bartolommeo at the time that I was their visitor. The picture in question, however, whatever may be the truth of this tradition, is a very ordinary painting.

Outside the refectory is a spacious vestibule, supplied with marble apparatus for washing, and towels, where the community assemble at the sound of the first dinner or supper bell, the refectory door not being opened until the second bell has been rung.

Over the entrance to the refectory of San Bartolommeo are placed the arms of the Barnabite order: a cross with the letters P A on either side. One day, when the community were assembling in the vestibule before dinner, I asked one of them what these letters signified, to which he replied, laughingly, that they meant 'Pane' and 'Acqua,' (bread and water), referring to the spare diet used in convents. He soon afterwards, however, added that this was

SAN BARTOLOMMEO DEGLI ARMENI. 11

only a joke on his part, and that the letters in question stood for the words "Paulus Apostolus," St. Paul being regarded as the patron of the order.

I may mention, in passing, that the Barnabite priest, who could be thus merry at a time of leisure and recreation, was a highly instructed man, and to his other attainments added a knowledge of English, which he had acquired by his own unaided efforts. He showed me a manuscript grammar of the English language, which he had arranged and written out himself, but having never had an opportunity of conversing in English, he was unable to speak it, although he could read it fairly.

The Chapter-room of this convent is a spacious, vaulted chamber, adorned with a few pictures, and surrounded on three sides by antiquated arm-chairs. Among the paintings are St. Pantaleon, patron of the medical art, and two full-length figures of St. Peter and St. Paul. This is not now, however, used as a Chapter-room, another and smaller chamber on the first floor being employed for that purpose.

The latter contains a series of portraits of notabilities of the Barnabite Order. The novitiate, or set of apartments reserved for the novices, and the master of the novices, consists of a floor above that used by the regular community, a large door at the foot of the staircase separating the two, as is usual in convents to which a novitiate is attached.

Having briefly described the conventual buildings of San Bartolommeo degli Armeni, it may now be proper to give some account of the ordinary daily routine observed by the community. It is necessary, however, first to mention, that the inmates of a religious house are divided into two bodies—the 'Padri,' or priests, and the 'Laici,' or lay-brothers. The lay-brothers are bound by the same vows as the priests, wear the same habit,* and are, in all

* The habit worn by the Barnabites is very similar to that of the other congregations of Regular Clerks, which bears, it is said, a close resemblance to the cassock used by the secular priests in the 16th century. The cassock is black, and without buttons in front, being confined instead by a sash round the

respects, as much part of the community as they, the difference between them being, that those who are to serve the convent in a spiritual capacity, receive holy orders, while those who minister to the temporal requirements of the brotherhood (that is, the lay-brothers), do not take priests' orders. The priests, as may be supposed, are usually far more instructed than the lay-brothers, although the latter, especially among the endowed orders, are often by no means illiterate.*

waist. They generally wear buckles to their shoes, and on the head a 'berretta,' or square cap, when at home, and a black three-cornered clerical hat out of doors. The lay-brothers do not wear the 'berretta,' but otherwise their habit is precisely the same as that of the priests, including the three-cornered hat.

* Monks and friars, who live in monasteries according to a given rule (Latin *regula*) are called the *regular clergy*, while parish priests and their curates are termed the *secular clergy*. There is, however, another important body of the secular clergy, consisting of the 'cappellani,' or chaplains, who for a fixed stipend celebrate mass daily in some church or chapel. These chaplaincies have usually been founded and en-

Each priest says mass early in the morning, at one of the altars of the church, after which he devotes about half an hour to meditation in the choir. He then returns from the church to the convent, and having first taken a cup of coffee, and a small piece of dry bread, spends the interval until mid-day in his own room, in writing, or in reading the breviary and other books. At noon, the church bell rings for the 'Ave Maria,' after which the dinner-bell sounds, and thereupon the community proceed to the Refectory. On entering it, they stand in two

dowed in a parochial, or other church, by deceased persons for the benefit of their souls, and they exist in large numbers all over Italy. The priests who hold them are considered as beneficed clergymen, without cure of souls; but their *status* is inferior to that of the parochial clergy, and they are styled simply "preti so and so." Some of the chaplaincies, even in convents, are occasionally filled by these secular chaplains; thus, at San Bartolommeo degli Armeni, there were two such chaplains, who had their lodgings near the convent, and came daily to celebrate mass in the church, in accordance with the intentions of the founders of their respective chaplaincies.

lines opposite to one another, whilst the Superior (styled among the Barnabites, 'Padre Provosto,' or 'Father Provost,') says grace in Latin. They then take their respective seats and begin their meal. This invariably commences with 'minestra,' or soup. Bouilli, called in Italian, 'lesso,' is next served; and afterwards a small portion of meat, generally, roasted, called 'umido'—a name given in Italy to any dish of meat served with gravy. Dinner concludes with a little dessert, such as a couple of apples, or an orange, or a few grapes, for each person.

The food is excellent in quality, and well cooked. It is served out in portions in the kitchen, whence it is conveyed to the refectory, every person's portion being placed on the table in front of him, to be taken or left at his option. Their beverage is the wine of the country. During dinner, or at least a part of it, a Latin devotional book is read aloud. Whilst I was at the convent, the public reading at meals was from a commentary on St. Paul, preceded each time by a few verses from one of

St. Paul's epistles. When they have finished, the Superior rising, says, 'Andiamo' (let us go), and all again forming in two lines, grace is said, after which they indulge in half an hour's 'recreazione,' or recreation, either in the Chapter-room or the garden, according to the season of the year. They then retire to their rooms until three o'clock, when they are summoned by sound of bell into choir, there to spend half an hour in silent meditation. The remainder of the afternoon and evening is devoted to reading the breviary and other books, writing, hearing confessions, and any business they may have to transact.

At nine o'clock the bell rings for supper. Grace is said with the same formalities as at dinner. Supper, in Italian 'cena,' comprises nearly the same fare as the mid-day meal, except that one of the two meat dishes is omitted. On fast days they dispense with the piece of dry bread that is taken on other mornings, drinking only a cup of coffee without milk. Dinner on fast days differs from that on ordinary days, chiefly in fish being eaten instead of meat;

SAN BARTOLOMMEO DEGLI ARMENI. 17

and in lieu of supper, a light meal called 'colezione' (collation) is served, consisting of a single dish of boiled vegetables, followed by the slender dessert of fruit already described. It must be borne in mind, that at every meal each person had only an allotted portion—and that a small one—of the several dishes, so that the quantity of food allowed was much less than might be supposed from an enumeration of the dishes.*

---

* Though I have had several hundred meals in Italian monasteries, I have never seen butter used but once, and on that occasion it was served at dinner as one of the dishes of the day. This was at San Bartolommeo. At the same convent, on another occasion, one of the dishes consisted of boiled eggs, two of which were served out to each person. These were eaten without the aid of a spoon. My inveterate English habits, however, induced me to ask the lay-brother for one, a request at which he was apparently a little puzzled. He hesitated for a moment, and then left the refectory, returning shortly with a large tablespoon, which with mingled Italian courtesy and grace he placed before me, evidently without suspecting the use to be made of it.

After supper, another half hour is spent in recreation, from which the community are summoned at ten, into choir for prayer. This, the concluding devotional exercise of the day, commences with a private examination of conscience, more particularly in regard to the actions of the past day. This examination of conscience is, of course, conducted in silence, and is called 'Esame,' or examination. On its termination, a few prayers are recited, and lastly, the Superior sprinkles the choir with holy water, and dismisses the fraternity for the night with his benediction. This practice of blessing the assembled choir with holy water by the Superior, at the close of the day, prevails in convents generally, and has an impressive effect. Then, leaving the church, they proceed to their respective rooms, every person holding a lighted taper, and each entering his own chamber as he comes to it, in unbroken silence.

On Sundays, there were additional services in the morning and evening, with a sermon at both; and although San Bartolommeo is not a parish church, it was attended on these occa-

SAN BARTOLOMMEO DEGLI ARMENI. 19

sions by a large congregation. A curious custom with regard to preaching exists in this and some other churches in Genoa, which may be worth mentioning. There are two pulpits, one on either side of the church, and at the afternoon sermon on Sunday, these are occupied respectively by two priests, one of whom addresses his hearers for a few minutes in Italian, and then the second preacher translates the substance of what has been said into the popular *patois*, called 'Genovese.' The first speaker then resumes his discourse, to be again followed by the second priest in the vernacular dialect; and this is repeated several times. The afternoon sermon in San Bartolommeo was preceded by catechetical instruction of the children.

It is a pretty sight in Italian churches, in warm weather, to see the wave-like effect produced by the constant use of their fans by the feminine part of the congregation, especially in Genoa, where the general substitution of the Pezzoto, or long veil, for the bonnet, adds to the effect of this southern practice. I have noticed it particularly in the little church of San Bartolommeo, which, when crowded with worshippers on a Sunday in summer, has, owing to the custom in question, quite a gay Spanish-like appearance.

The systematic life, of which I have endeavoured to convey some idea, is observed day after day, and year after year, every portion of the day's routine being governed by an exact rule; although this rule varies slightly according to the season of the year. The whole of the monastic routine is regulated by the sound of the convent-bell. Indeed, the continual ringing of bells for one purpose or another, is among the peculiar characteristics of conventual life. Another of the characteristics that distinguish this manner of life from ordinary secular life, is the absence of any common room for the community to meet together; for, except in the refectory, and the short half hour of recreation after meals, they do not assemble for conversation or otherwise, passing most of their time in their respective rooms. These chambers, as has been already said, open into a passage or corridor, called in conventual phrase, a dormitory. The principal dormitory at San Bartolommeo is broad and lofty, and is adorned by several paintings. Placed against one of its walls is a *prie-dieu*, with forms of prayer written over it in Latin, to be said by the community whenever they go out from, or return to, the convent.

The complete silence that prevailed was very striking, recalling to the mind the quiet of country life rather than the proximity of a great city. Except when the convent bell summoned the community to the church or the refectory, the only sounds heard were an occasional footstep along the pavement of the dormitory, or the closing of one of the cell doors which, in the general silence, would resound through the old monastic buildings. Sometimes, too, might be distinguished the measured tread of a black-robed priest, slowly pacing up and down the vaulted corridor, with breviary in hand, reading the office prescribed by his church for daily recitation by the clergy. On looking out of my window over Genoa and the blue Mediterranean beyond, I could often descry one or two of the monks taking exercise in the pretty convent garden, or a small knot of them playing a game with the wooden balls which I have already mentioned as a favourite pastime among the inmates of religious houses.

But of all the parts of monastic life, and of all the various striking effects associated with it, none was to my mind so impressive as the meeting together of the community in the choir, at the close of the day, for silent meditation—a practice which, though I first became acquainted with it at San Bartolommeo, I found to be common to most, if not to all, religious Orders. Around the choir, each in his separate stall in private prayer, sat or knelt the whole community; the flickering oil lamp, by which alone the church was preserved from total darkness, adding by its "dim religious light," and the indistinctness of its effect, to the impressive character of the scene. For impressive it could hardly fail to appear to most unprejudiced minds.

Serious self-communion, involving an examination of the conscience generally, and of the actions and feelings of the day in particular, must necessarily be a solemn act, whatever may be the doctrinal opinions of him who performs it. And this self-communion, while it lies at the root of the theory of monastic life, has been embodied in the rules laid down by all the founders of religious Orders; and, so far as my opportunities of observation went, it seems to form an important part of the actual practice of the religious communities of Italy.

Occasionally, some one or other of the community of this and other convents where I have sojourned, would enter into a theological discussion with me. But this was not very often the case; for, as it was well known that I disagreed with the Roman Church on questions of doctrine, religious controversy was for the most part avoided on both sides. When, however, such discussions did arise, they were invariably conducted with good temper, and not without argumentative skill on the part of my opponents.

I could not but feel surprised at being asked,

on one or two occasions (although not at San Bartolommeo), whether the Church of England admits the doctrine of the Atonement, implying, as the question did, such entire ignorance of the religious sentiments of the large majority of English Protestants, although, perhaps, not greater ignorance than is manifested of Roman Catholic opinion by many zealous Protestants. The truth appears to be, that half-educated persons on either side, instead of making the most of their common Christianity, will often barely allow to one another the character of Christians at all.

As in judging of individual character, small traits are often more important than the apparently greater actions of a man's life, so, to enable the reader to form a correct idea of conventual life, as it actually is, it may be desirable to mention some matters which, though of minor importance, and, indeed, when taken singly, insignificant in themselves, nevertheless constitute not unimportant elements in the picture I am endeavouring to draw of monasticism in Italy.

Among such secondary matters, for example, is the simplicity and scantiness of the household furniture in convents, and the comparative absence of what in England are understood by domestic comforts. Thus, fireplaces and carpets are, so far as my experience goes, unknown in Italian convents. To guard against cold, however, some Orders, such as the Barnabites, wear a stouter cassock in winter than in summer; and, occasionally, a rough earthenware vase, with a little charcoal, just sufficient to warm the fingers, is used by some of the older and infirm brethren. Nor have I ever seen looking-glasses among the articles of furniture in a monastery, and have always had to provide myself with one. Some of the monks and friars have small tin boxes containing a piece of very indifferent glass, such as may be bought at a toy-booth at a fair for a few halfpence. I remember, on two occasions, once at San Bartolommeo, and once at the Capuchin convent of Campi, having such a primitive form of mirror lent me by members of the respective communities.

Great attention is paid to cleanliness in the convents with which I am acquainted. They are usually thoroughly cleaned every Saturday. In the Mendicant Orders, each friar sweeps out his own cell, leaving the dust outside his cell door; and any one, walking along the corridors on a Saturday morning, may see a little heap of rubbish at the door of every cell, which is carried away by a lay-brother, when he sweeps the corridor, and sprinkles it with water. I may here add that in friaries of the barefooted Orders, there is no such process as cleaning of shoes, for the reason that no shoes are worn; but it is otherwise in the Endowed Orders, in which shoes are worn and cleaned, as in secular houses.

In the matter of diet there is a marked difference between most of the Endowed Orders ('Possidenti,' as they are called in Italy), and the Mendicants. For not only is the fare of the begging friar more sparing in quantity, but it is far coarser in quality, and less well cooked than in the generality of the richer Orders. Thus, although the fasts and abstinences were most strictly observed at San Bartolommeo, and the quantity of food taken by the community at all times very small compared with English notions of what is required for the sustenance of healthy men, still the table was much better served than in the convents of Mendicants which I subsequently visited. Table-cloths also were used, and the dinner service and other requisites for the table were such as might be seen in an ordinary gentleman's house. The chambers or cells of the 'Possidenti' are, moreover, usually much larger than the tiny cells of the friars; and the former, as a general rule, use linen wearing apparel, which is wholly dispensed with by some, at least, if not by most of the Mendicant Orders.

This difference in the diet and habits of the less rigorous among the Endowed Orders and the Mendicants, is aptly illustrated by a remark made to me by the Guardian, or Superior, of the large Capuchin convent at Rome, when I presented my letter of introduction, and requested the privilege of residing, for a short time, at the convent. Among other objections which he urged, he said that the manner of life observed in monasteries would be too rigid for me. I answered that I had just been spending several weeks with the Barnabites at Genoa, to which the Guardian replied, "Si, ma sono Signori, i Barnabiti! Noi altri, al contrario, siamo poveri Mendicanti." ("Yes, but the Barnabites are gentlemen, whereas, we are poor mendicants.") He did, however, finally consent to receive me as a visitor; and of my highly interesting sojourn at his convent, a detailed account will be given in a subsequent chapter.

CHAPTER II.

Genoa and its Convents, continued—Journey to Rome.

VENICE alone excepted, I know no city of Italy more picturesque than Genoa, and none that brings before you so vividly the idea of one of the great republics of mediæval Italy. For not only are there a score of points of view, each of which would form a charming picture, but owing to its extensive trading enterprise, Genoa unites a large population and cheerful prosperity to a thoroughly mediæval and artistic character, thus recalling to the mind the busy activity of the Genoa of the sixteenth century, as well as the picturesqueness which it shared with most other towns of the period. As you thread its narrow winding old streets, lofty houses rising on either side, but with so little space between them as almost to admit of a person joining hands with another on the opposite side of the way. you meet rows of well-packed mules carrying their merchandise to or from the crowded port. Many of these streets are paved with flag stones, and are impervious to carriages, while others are of steep ascent, being built up the base of the fine amphitheatre of mountains at the foot of which Genoa stands.

Besides its numerous alley-like streets, Genoa possesses two or three of wider and more modern construction, such as the Strada Nuova, and the Strada Carlo Felice. The former consists wholly of palaces, and is so exceedingly elegant, that the Emperor Joseph II is said to have declared that it ought to have been enclosed by iron gates, being too beautiful to be used as a common thoroughfare. The highly artistic and picturesque effect of the palatial and domestic architecture of Genoa is increased by the practice, so general there, of painting the outside of the houses in fresco, sometimes to represent figures, and sometimes only with plain colours tastefully arranged.

The stately palaces of Genoa, and their galleries of paintings are well known. There are also numerous churches, many of them exceedingly elegant, for besides the cathedral and the Annunziata, which all travellers visit, the churches of Santa Maria in Carignano and La Madonna delle Vigne (both of them collegiate churches of secular canons), Sant' Ambrogio, San Sisto, San Filippo Neri, San Matteo, and others, are well worth seeing. Genoa is likewise adorned by several pretty piazzas, the principal of which are those of Sant' Ambrogio, Le Fontane Amorose, and San Matteo, the last of which is celebrated by Rogers in his "Italy." Not the least of the effective points of view at Genoa are those to be obtained of the mountains in the distance as seen through the vista of some of the narrow streets leading in that direction.

But it is from the mountain heights themselves behind Genoa, that the finest view of this grand old city is to be had. Tower and spire of church and convent rise, thickly studded, among the mass of building beneath you, while the busy port, and the blue Mediterranean beyond, together with the Riviera mountains to the west, and the lofty peak of Porto Fino eastwards, complete a varied and most striking picture. It is, however, with the numerous monasteries of Genoa that we are here chiefly concerned, and to these we will now return.

Genoa is often called the City of Palaces. It might with equal truth be termed the city of convents, so numerous are the monasteries of both sexes comprised within the town and its immediate neighbourhood. During my sojourn at San Bartolommeo, I went over several other monasteries. Among these was the Oratorian house of San Filippo, where I accidentally made the acquaintance of one of the Oratorian Fathers, Padre C——, who, to other accomplishments, added that of speaking English. The Oratorians are a congregation of secular priests instituted by St. Philip Neri in the sixteenth century. They are called secular priests, because notwithstanding that they live in community, and according to a monastic rule, they do not take perpetual vows and may accordingly leave their convents if they wish, although I believe this privilege is seldom exercised. The Oratorians of San Filippo have a handsome and apparently a well endowed convent. Indeed its appearance externally, as well as internally, is almost palatial. Their church is splendidly decorated with painting and gilding, and has a particularly beautiful pavement made of marble of various colours.

Padre C—— introduced me to a Carmelite friar, Padre B———, of the Convent of San Carlo in the Strada Balbi. There are two branches of the Carmelite Order; the unreformed branch, commonly called in Italy "Carmelitani calzi," or "shoe-wearing Carmelites;" and the reformed Carmelites, following St. Teresa's reform, and known as "Carmelitani scalzi," *i.e.* "barefooted." The latter are also popularly called "Teresiani," from St. Teresa, their founder. The friars at San Carlo belong to this branch. Their habit is made of brown cloth over which, when the weather requires it, they wear a white cloak. They have a three-cornered hat of white felt, similar, except in colour, to those worn by secular priests; but this they often dispense with, using either a hood, or if the season be warm and dry, no covering whatever for the head. Like many monastic churches in Italy, San Carlo is parochial, one of the friars being the "parroco" or parish priest. Padre B— informed me that when this is the case, the bishop of the diocese has jurisdiction over the conventual church in matters strictly parochial; otherwise religious houses of men in Italy are wholly exempt from episcopal control, being subject only to that of the General of their respective Orders, who in most instances resides at Rome.

Padre B— was kind enough to offer to accompany me on the following day to another Carmelite convent, that of Santa Anna, situated on a steep hill behind Genoa. I was glad to accept this offer, being bent upon seeing as much as possible of Italian monastic life in all its phases. This was the first time I had walked out in company with a friar; indeed, Padre B— was the first friar I had known personally, and this circumstance, slight as it may appear, felt in itself a novelty; for it is one thing to read of, or even to see, hooded monks and friars, and another to be brought into actual intercourse with them, so different in many respects are both their character and their manners, to say nothing of their mediæval appearance, from that of other people.

Santa Anna is a large and rather handsome convent. I was offered coffee by the friars, and was pressed to accept a bottle of eau-de-cologne from the convent "farmacia" or pharmacy, where several friars were standing behind the counters preparing medecines. These conventual pharmacies are fitted up like a well-stored chemist's shop, with the addition of some symbol of religion, such as a small altar, or a crucifix, or an image of the Madonna.

That at Santa Maria Novella at Florence, for example, is celebrated, and is often visited by travellers. Attached to them are monastic apothecaries, that is to say, friars who have gone through their medical course at a university and have thus qualified themselves to practise in medicine and surgery. They are much consulted by the poor. Pharmacies are attached only to the chief monastery of each Order in every province, called the Provincial house, from its being the residence of the provincial or Superior of the Order throughout a given province.

One of the chief convents at Genoa is that of the Annunziata, whose splendid church enjoys almost a European reputation. This convent was, until within a few years, among the largest monasteries in the kingdom of Sardinia, but a considerable part of it had been recently appropriated by government for an educational college, including the handsome Cloister. Nevertheless, the convent is still large, and contained at the period of my visit fifty-two friars, who are of the Observant* branch of the Franciscan Order, wearing a dark brown habit and cowl, with a white cord round the waist, and sandals on the feet. I met in one of the corridors of this convent an aged and infirm friar, who was being led about for exercise by a younger member of the brotherhood. I was informed that he was ninety

* The Observants were founded by St. Bernardin of Sienna, about the year 1400. They were brought into England by Edward IV., who settled them at Greenwich, adjoining the royal residence there. Henry VII., by a Charter still extant, bearing date 1486, confirmed and augmented their privileges. Catherine of Arragon, the first wife of Henry VIII., was also a great benefactor of the Greenwich Observants, and it is related of her that she used to rise at midnight to join the friars at Matins. Their monastery having been re-opened by Queen Mary after the general suppression of the religious houses by Henry VIII., was finally suppressed by Queen Elizabeth on June 12th, 1559.

The Observants are said to be the same order as

years old, and quite blind. The Conventual Church of the Annunziata is a magnificent building, and one of the most superb specimens existing of the practice, so general in Italy, of decorating churches by sumptuous and tasteful profusion of gilding and fresco painting. The whole of the gilding and of the frescoes in this splendid church had been renewed within the last eight years by the labour of a friar of the adjoining convent. When the sun sheds its rays over this glittering brilliancy of colour, and over the scarcely less brilliant mass of coloured marbles by which the church is adorned, the

that which in France was commonly called Cordeliers. The other chief branches of the Franciscans are the Conventuals, called in Italy 'Conventuali,' Capuchins, Recollects (known in Italy as ' Riformati') and Alcantarists. The three last mentioned Orders (and also a fourth, as I have heard, but of which I do not remember the name) are under the government of one and the same General, who resides at Rome in the Observant Convent of Santa Maria in Ara Cœli, on the Capitol. The remainder have a separate General, with no farther connexion with one another than their common profession of the rule of St. Francis.

effect is strikingly beautiful, especially as the interior of the edifice itself is architecturally very elegant, independent of its chromatic auxiliaries. The exterior is unfinished, but a Greek façade has lately been erected which is handsome, although not in unison with the Italian style of the interior.

Another highly interesting monastery that I visited, is the large Capuchin Convent of La Concezione near the Acqua Sola, or public garden of Genoa. When I went over it, the number of friars within its walls exceeded one hundred. This is the Provincial house of the extensive Capuchin province of Genoa, comprising some thirty-two or thirty-three houses of the Order. This convent being the chief house of the province, contains a hospital and surgery. One of the friars was famous for his skill in dental surgery, and as I happened to be suffering from toothache, I went to the convent to consult him. I found several persons waiting in the porch for advice, which was given in a chamber in close proximity to the convent gate. The friar-dentist appeared in his ordinary

monastic habit, and after examining my case
gave me such advice as he thought necessary.
These monastic surgeons and dentists in Italy
often enjoy a considerable reputation, especially
among the poor, who consult them free of expense.

It has been already explained that the immediate background of Genoa consists of lofty
hills, on the summits of which (or high up on
their sides) many convents have been erected at
various times. Among these are the convents
of La Maddelena and San Nicola, both belonging to Austin Friars, and a monastery of
Observants, called La Madonna dell' Origine.
The Austin Friars, or Augustinians, are altogether distinct from the Regular Canons of St.
Austin, which Order still exists in many parts
of Italy, and indeed at Genoa itself. The
Regular Canons are an endowed Order (that is to
say they possess revenues instead of being
mendicants) and their monasteries for the most
part have the rank and title of abbeys. The
Augustinian Friars, on the contrary, are mendicants, and their convents are therefore gene-

rally poor and simple. Their habit consists of
a black cassock and a sort of cape of the same
colour, ending in a point behind. They wear
either a black hood or a three-cornered felt hat
over the head. The Order is divided into two
branches, the reformed branch, called " scalzi,"
or bare-footed; and the unreformed, called
" calzi," or shoe-wearing. They have each their
separate General, and are altogether independent of one another. This is generally the case
where an Order has been reformed. The reformer did not attempt to introduce his reform
into the already existing monasteries of the
Order. He obtained leave from the Pope to
found a new branch, professing indeed the old
'rule' of the Order to which the reformer happened to belong, but with the addition of certain
special 'constitutions,' as they are called, intended
to provide for the more rigid enforcement of
the original rule. The new branch thus founded
was said to be 'reformed,' to distinguish it
from the old stock, or parent branch. This
system of restoring the severity of monastic
discipline by means of reformed branches of

existing Orders, prevailed to a greater extent formerly than in more recent times, when it has apparently become the practice to found entirely new and distinct Orders, rather than reforms of the old. Thus we do not now hear of fresh reforms, or branches, of the Benedictines, Carthusians, Franciscans, or Augustinians, independent Orders being founded instead, such as the Redemptorists, Passionists, and others.

The Convent of La Maddelena is perched on a lofty hill behind Genoa, and is of the Augustinian Order, and if my memory is not at fault, it is of the reformed branch, or "Agostiniani scalzi." The church is remarkable for a subterranean chapel, and for the prodigious number of relics it contains. The walls are formed of large wooden panels, which, on being opened, exhibit innumerable bones and other relics preserved within glass cases. When I visited this convent, one Fra Carlo, a friar, lived there, who worked beautifully in ivory. He showed me a certificate from which it appeared that the medal for the ivory carving at the Great Exhibition of New York had been awarded to him. The view over Genoa from the heights near La Maddelena is very striking. There is also a convent at Genoa of the other branch of the Augustinians, called La Madonna della Consolazione. Its church is parochial, one of the friars being the parish priest. The monastery contains a dormitory, or corridor with the cells opening into it, which on account of its immense length is worth seeing. At the time of my visit it contained thirty-five friars.

I likewise went to see the Dominican Convent of Castello. The Dominicans are friars, and their Order was instituted by St. Dominic in the 13th century. They have practically ceased to be mendicants, that is, they do not live on begging alms, and are, apparently, among the most flourishing of the religious Orders. Their dress consists of a white habit, over which a black cloak is generally worn. They wear a three-cornered black hat, like many of the monastic orders. They have a somewhat exceptional method of celebrating mass, differing in several minor points from the ordinary

Liturgy of the Roman Church. The Dominicans (who are also known by the name of the Order of Preachers) do not eat meat during any part of the year, unless it be prescribed medically, in which case they dine apart from the rest of the community. In all Dominican convents that I have seen, there is a small chamber or ante-room adjoining the refectory, for the use of those in whose favour the rule prohibiting meat is dispensed with on medical grounds. The Superior of a Dominican convent bears the title of Prior, the convents of the Order having the rank and style of priories.

Two other religious houses that I went over during my first visit to Genoa, deserve particular mention. On an eminence, almost overlooking the railway station, is a monastery of Minims. Several of the religious Orders having adopted, as a sign of humility, the appellation of Minori, such as " Cappucini Minori," and " Osservanti Minori," these assume the superlative form of " Minimi," by way of expressing a yet lower degree of humility. They wear a black habit, and they abstain altogether, as I was informed, not only from meat, but also from milk, eggs, butter and cheese.

Padre C——., the Oratorian, accompanied me in my visit to this convent, together with a friend of his, an Italian gentleman of great religious zeal, and the relation of a cardinal at Rome, to whom, subsequently, he gave me a letter of introduction. Whilst we were toiling up the ascent leading to the monastery, this gentleman asked the Oratorian of what use was such extreme severity of discipline, considering that the Catholic Church does not hold it to be essential to salvation. The priest replied that doubtless the Church would not have sanctioned the rules of this, or any other Order, without having a wise purpose in view; but beyond this, he did not enter into the wide question which the layman had, perhaps unconsciously, raised by his inquiry.

Not far distant from the Minims, is a house of Lazarist Fathers, originally a French Order, and called in Italy "Signori della Missione," from the missionary objects with which the Order was instituted. It was founded by St.

Vincent of Paula, as a congregation of secular priests, under the name of "Congregatio Missionum," and derives its name of Lazarists from the fact of the parent house at Paris having been dedicated to St. Lazarus.

Genoa contains numerous convents of women, although, in regard to these, not having been able, of course, to visit them in person, my information is made up of gleanings from various second-hand sources. In the case of monasteries of men, I have, as far as possible, acted on the principle of stating only such facts concerning them as I have actually seen, or have heard from members of the same Order, in respect of which they are stated; but I was necessarily unable to obtain similar opportunities of acquiring information about convents of women. And here it may be well to observe that the word monastery, in Italian, "monastero," may be used generally for any religious house whatever. The word convent, in Italian "convento," has a like general signification. But "monastero" is more particularly employed to denote a religious house of *women*, and also of monks strictly so called; such as Benedictines, Cistercians, Carthusians, and Regular Canons, while "convento" is most often applied to houses of friars, as Franciscans, Augustinians, Carmelites, and Dominicans, or of Regular Clerks, as Barnabites and Theatins. Thus the word "convento" is, in practice, used in a wider sense than "monastero," which is generally (though not necessarily) applied to nunneries, or to the habitations of monks proper, as distinguished from friars, &c. When, however, "un monastero" simply is spoken of, a convent of nuns is almost always meant. "Monastero di ———" so and so, is frequently inscribed over nunneries. Nuns, too, of all kinds, are called "monache," the feminine plural form of "monaco," a monk.

Among the many monasteries of women at Genoa, are the Augustinians, Poor Clares, Dominicanesses, Regular Canonesses, two of the Santissima Annunziata, commonly known by the name of 'Le Turchine' (blue), from the colour of their habit, the Brignole nuns, and very many others. Of these, some are cloistered and others uncloistered.

Religious Orders of nuns are said to be cloistered when they live a life of strict enclosure within their convents, while those who are uncloistered are less closely confined, and are generally devoted to works of charity, or to tuition.

In some instances, nuns may take vows for a limited period. This is the case in one of the most flourishing convents in Genoa, that belonging to the Brignole nuns; so called from a Marquis Brignole, their founder. Signor R—., a Genoese lawyer, told me that a friend of his physician had married a Brignole nun after the expiration of her monastic vows, which had been taken for five years. He added that this quondam nun is now the mother of six children.

During a second and longer visit to Genoa in the following year, I had the opportunity of seeing many more convents of which some account will be given in a subsequent chapter.

As I wished to arrive at Rome in time for the ceremonies of the Holy Week, I was with regret compelled to take leave of my friends at San Bartolommeo, after a residence of several weeks in their convent, of which I shall ever retain a most pleasing recollection.

I took the steamboat for Civita Vecchia, leaving gay and picturesque Genoa on a Sunday evening, when the streets were so thronged by people promenading for pleasure, as to present the appearance of some grand *festa*, although it was but an ordinary Sunday. We arrived at the pretty little seaport of Civita Vecchia on Tuesday morning, having touched at Leghorn for eight hours.

I had now, for the first time, set foot within the patrimony of St. Peter. Everywhere you see the old papal arms of the tiara and cross-keys; and you often meet with Latin inscriptions, headed by the name of some Pope with whom you are familiar in history, but with whom you feel, as it were, brought into more intimate acquaintance by reading what was written while the historical personage was actually living.

One of the first of these that attracted my attention at Civita Vecchia, was an inscription inside a building bearing the name of Julius II., the warrior-pontiff. This name carries the mind back to the days when the papal power was still at its zenith, immediately preceding the great blow it was soon to receive by the Reformation — to the days when our own Henry VII. was erecting monasteries and churches of the old religion, which were destined to be so speedily converted to the purposes of the new faith.

The distance from Civita Vecchia to Rome was then traversed in eight hours by diligence, and in ten or eleven by vetturini. The general character of the country is flat and monotonous, but the latter portion is more varied, some parts of it being both hilly and wooded. It was a bright moonlight night on which I approached the Eternal City. I remember the feelings I experienced on obtaining my first glimpse of Rome, when the stately dome of St.

Peter's, lit up by the silvery moonbeams, rose majestically to the view, and when passing soon afterwards under the old gateway, I realized the fact that I was actually within the city itself. The ponderous old gate, however, was not opened until sundry heavy blows, directed against it, had aroused the sleepy guards within.

CHAPTER IV.

Holy Week at Rome.

ROME produces the impression of being built over a large extent of generally flat ground, bounded by lofty walls and massive gateways. The "seven hills" are soon ascertained, but their size and elevation are not such as to render it otherwise than a practically correct description of Rome, to say that it stands mostly on level ground. It is intersected by the Tiber, the views from the bridges crossing which, together with the principal piazzas and the elegant though narrow Corso, form some of the most interesting points of the modern city. Persons who visit Rome chiefly for its remains of classical times, or for its galleries of sculpture and painting, or for its ecclesiastical monuments, can hardly fail to find their highest expectations realized. And those who are fortunate enough to combine a taste for each of these different objects of interest will enjoy a two or threefold intellectual pleasure. My lot was cast among the latter. I longed to examine what time had bequeathed to us of Imperial Rome, to obtain a personal knowledge of its temples, its circus, its triumphal arches, its noble columns, its tombs, its viaducts. I desired also to become acquainted with those beautiful efforts of the Roman chisel which modern Europe admires without being able to equal, and those not less beautiful works of art, the exquisite productions of the great masters of painting in the middle ages. At the same time, I was glad to avail myself of the opportunity that happened to be thrown in my path, of gaining a practical insight into one of the leading institutions of a church that has exercised so important an influence on the history of the world as the Church of Rome. But although during a sojourn of several months at Rome, I found a vast deal to interest me and of a very varied kind, I do not

intend to inflict upon the reader a detailed
account of my round of sight-seeing. The
remains of classical Rome, and also the galleries
of sculpture and painting by which the modern
city is enriched, have been so often described,
that I shall confine myself almost exclusively
to the subject on which I had unusual opportunities of obtaining information, viz., the
monastic system as it actually exists at Rome.
Other matters will be occasionally touched upon,
but they will occupy a subordinate place to the
main purpose of this volume.

During my first visit to Rome I enjoyed the
rare advantage of residing in a large convent
of Capuchin friars—La Madonna della Concezione—in the Piazza Barberini. For this
privilege I was indebted to a good introduction
I brought from Genoa, which, however, barely
sufficed to induce the Superior to receive me as
a visitor, it being unusual to admit any visitors
in convents, more especially in the case of
persons who are not members of the Church
of Rome. I went with the intention of remaining only a fortnight, but protracted my

stay from time to time, until three months had elapsed before I bade farewell to my monastic hosts.

I had hastened forward with the intention of reaching Rome in time to be present at the ceremonies of the Holy Week. These commenced a few days after my arrival, and I will now (retaining the order of time in which my Roman experiences were acquired) endeavour to give the reader some idea, although a most inadequate one, of the far-famed religious services by which the week of Christ's Passion is celebrated at the Papal Court.

It is scarcely necessary to premise that these ceremonies must be seen in order to be fully understood. So many of their effects are musical, while others are of the nature of beautiful and impressive sights that it would not be easy for even the most graphic description to do justice to the subject. All, therefore, that I can attempt, is to assist the reader in forming some conception, however imperfect, of the imposing ceremonials to behold which thousands of Protestants as well as Catholics, visit Rome annually.

The ceremonies of the Holy Week are intended to commemorate, and in a certain sense to dramatise, the several parts of the Passion of Christ. Like other christian communions, the Church of Rome commemorates the anniversary of that grand event by special services; but besides a simple commemoration of the incidents attending the crucifixion, the liturgy of the Roman Catholic church seems to throw them into a form approaching to a religious drama, with the object, it would appear, of making the people realize more vividly the mysteries of the Saviour's Passion. Thus, the liturgy does not merely speak of, or commemorate, these as events long since enacted, but implies by the general tenor of its language and ceremonial that they are happening at the present time, and that the "faithful" are actually witnesses of them. On Palm Sunday, for example, the procession of palms, in which the Pope is carried in his chair of state, holding a palm branch in his hand, is a sort of

PALM SUNDAY.

dramatic representation of the triumphal entry into Jerusalem. The office of Tenebræ (during which is sung the celebrated " Miserere" of the Sistine Chapel) is so called from the lights being extinguished to denote the darkness that pervaded the earth at the Crucifixion.

And the same idea—that of dramatising the Passion—runs through other portions of the Holy Week ceremonies. The feeling, then, with which these services are supposed to be attended is that of deep sympathy with the Saviour in the several parts of his Passion. Persons who witness them only as pageants are sometimes disappointed, for the ceremonies in question are not intended as mere worldly shows. Whatever temporal state and pageantry may accompany them is, professedly, secondary to the religious feeling that lies below their surface; and to ignore the latter is to leave out that to which the external pomp is indebted for its life and spirit.

On the morning of Palm Sunday, the first day of Holy Week, I proceeded to St. Peter's, and although it was not yet eight o'clock when I set out, the streets already presented an appearance of unusual animation, from the long line of carriages and foot passengers hurrying towards the Basilica. Crossing the elegant bridge of St. Angelo, with the round castle or tower of the same name facing you on the opposite bank of the river, you turn to the left, and soon arrive in front of St. Peter's church. The Piazza di San Pietro is in itself an imposing sight. With the splendid church at one end, and at each side a handsome semi-circular colonnade, two beautiful fountains in the centre, and the Vatican palace close at hand, the *coup d'œil* is very striking. The Holy Week ceremonies being the principal subject of the present chapter, it may be well to defer the description of St. Peter's itself until I have to speak of it in its order among the churches of Rome. I will content myself with observing here that the great size, the admirable proportions, and the richness of colouring reflected from the variegated marbles with which the whole edifice is incrusted, and the numerous mosaics by which it is embellished, add in a high degree,

PALM SUNDAY.

to the effect of those parts of the Holy Week offices that are performed within its magnificent walls.

It would be difficult to describe adequately the imposing ceremonial of Palm Sunday. As the procession entered through the Chapel of the Sacrament, there issued from the papal choir a chorus of exquisite harmony, while the Pope was carried in a chair of state—the Sedia Gestatoria—raised aloft, and borne along the splendid nave of St. Peter's by half a score of attendants dressed in red silk, preceded by a long array of clergy, prelates and cardinals, the latter wearing superb white satin chasubles over purple cassocks and lace surplices. The Pope wore an ordinary episcopal mitre, and a scarlet velvet cope embroidered with gold over a white lace surplice. He sat on a throne, raised on a dais behind the high altar, and at right angles to it. On each side of the throne stood several dignitaries in finely wrought copes, and upon seats at either side of the choir sat the cardinals, prelates and other officials.

The effect was increased by the glittering helmets and uniforms of the noble Guards— the "Guardia Nobile"—who lined the choir; and by those of the Swiss Guards, as well as by the full-dress uniforms of officers of all nations present as spectators.

The brilliant scene produced by this variety of rich vestments, military as well as ecclesiastical, was heightened by the red cloth and velvet drapery with which the walls of the choir were hung. During the distribution of the palms, the long line of clergy advanced slowly, one by one, to receive a palm-branch from the Pope, after kissing his hand. There were the cardinals in purple cassocks, lace surplices, satin chasubles worked with gold, and scarlet skull-caps; prelates in copes also embroidered with gold, others in purple chasubles or in plain red robes; a fourth set of dignitaries wearing handsome ermine tippets, then the inferior clergy dressed in lace surplices; and lastly a brilliant array of officers in glittering uniforms. Little calculated as this meagre description is, to do justice to the scene, it may be conceived that the *tout-*

ensemble was splendid in itself, and rendered doubly so by the magnificence of the building in which the ceremonial was performed.

After the distribution of the palms, the procession was formed, all carrying palm branches in their hands. The Pope was borne in the chair of state down the nave, and outside the church, through the great door, the choir singing the fine anthems appointed in the Roman liturgy for this occasion. On the return of the procession, the cardinal-vicar (who is the Pope's immediate representative) celebrated Pontifical Mass at the high altar. The chaunting of the Passion of Christ from the Gospel of St. Mathew, in three solo parts (except that of the Jewish crowd which is given in chorus) was particularly beautiful. At the end of mass, the Pope gave the benediction from the throne. The exterior of St. Peter's presented a striking sight as the throng of people, issuing from its portals, descended the splendid marble steps, equal in breadth to the church itself, and the Piazza was soon filled by a great concourse of persons on foot, besides a large number of carriages, and masses of soldiers occupying one side of the square. As the sun shone and the fountains played in the midst of this numerous and motley assembly the effect was most gay and brilliant. Scarcely less so was the passage over the Bridge of St. Angelo amid a line of spectators on each side of the cardinals' and other prelates' carriages, of which there must have been nearly a hundred, exclusive of those of the general public.

The second office in celebration of the Holy Week, is known by the name of *Tenebræ*, and takes place on Wednesday afternoon in the Capella Sistina, the Pope's private chapel in the Vatican palace. The appellation of Tenebræ, darkness, is derived, as above observed, from the gradual extinguishing of the candles, placed in form of a triangle upon a tall candelabra, used only at this service, as well as of those on the altar.

The service itself—that is, the Liturgy used on the occasion—is the ordinary Matins for the day from the Roman Breviary, in which the Matins for the three last days of Holy Week are called " Matutinum Tenebrarum," on account of the ancient practice of putting out the lights. But the music sung is quite exceptional, being in harmony with the solemn season of Christ's Passion, and performed with exquisite skill and effect.

The Sistine Chapel is elegant in its proportions, and is enriched by Michael Angelo's celebrated fresco of the Last Judgment, which is conceived in the spirit of solemn grandeur, and executed on the immense scale that are among his chief characteristics. The Pope and cardinals were present in state. The papal choir ("cappella papale," as it is termed) enjoys a European celebrity for the style of vocal music it performs, and for the rare excellence of its execution. I believe the choir does not much exceed a score of performers, while some of the most striking musical effects it produces are sung by much fewer voices. It is one of the peculiarities of this choir that it is unaccompanied by an organ or other instrument. In St. Peter's itself, on Palm and Easter Sundays, and other great festivals, the organ remains silent when the papal choir performs. They cultivate such precision of vocal music, and produce such fine effects by delicate combinations of the human voice, that it is thought many of the finer shades of expression would otherwise be lost. The performance on the present occasion was very beautiful.

The Lamentations of Jeremiah, at the commencement of the office of Tenebræ, forming the first three Lessons of the day, were sung in solo with pathetic beauty, giving full vent to the sentiment contained in them; viz., the Prophet's lamentations over Jerusalem, transferred to the Church's lamentations for the passion and death of her Founder. The Miserere, at the end of the service—to which perhaps the papal choir is mainly indebted for its European reputation—was performed with extraordinary beauty and effect, increasing in grandeur and sublimity, amid the gradual extinction of the candles, until at its close you are left in a "dim religious light," which is supposed to harmonise with those feelings of sorrow and sympathy for the death of the

Redeemer, to which these services are intended to give rise.

On the following morning, Maunday, or Mandy Thursday, I again attended at the Sistine to hear the Pontifical Mass celebrated by a cardinal in the presence of the Pope. At its conclusion, a procession was formed, in which the Pope, accompanied by the cardinals, carried the Host to the Pauline Chapel in the Vatican, which had been prepared for its reception, and where among countless wax lights, and an uninterrupted succession of worshippers, it was to be solemnly kept until Good Friday. The Pope then proceeded to the "Loggia," or gallery over the west entrance of St. Peter's, to pronounce his blessing over the assembled multitude; but I was not present, as I hastened to secure a good position within the church for witnessing the interesting ceremony that followed immediately afterwards, in which the Pope washed the feet of some thirteen persons, in obedience to the command given by Christ, when he washed the feet of the Apostles at the Last Supper. Hence this ceremony is known by the name of "Mandatum"—"Mandatum do vobis," &c., which led to the day whereon it is performed being called Mandy, or Maunday Thursday. The thirteen persons whose feet were to be washed, were seated side by side on a bench in the south transept of St. Peter's, and clothed in white, including a curiously shaped cap of the same colour. The Pope then washed the feet of each person, a basin of water being held for him by an attendant, after which he dried them with a towel, and kissed them.

The Cena, which is celebrated on the termination of the Mandatum, in the spacious Loggia, or gallery over the vestibule of St. Peter's, is a very pretty and interesting scene. Here again, with a view of bringing vividly before the mind the various incidents of the Passion, and also to inculcate a practical lesson of humility and brotherly love, a sort of dramatic spectacle is exhibited, representing the Last Supper, or rather recalling that solemn event to our remembrance, for there is no attempt to imitate the details of the Gospel narrative, the ceremony consisting merely of the Pope serving at table the same persons whose feet he had previously washed. A long narrow table was laid out for supper with much taste and elegance, containing among other ornaments, handsome gold vases full of fragrant flowers; and the thirteen guests being seated along one side of it, the Pope walked several times up and down the opposite side, serving each guest with what he required.

In the afternoon of the same day I again heard the office of Tenebræ at the Sistine, which was in its general character similar to that of yesterday, although different music was performed. After the service, the Pope, accompanied by several cardinals and other dignitaries, left the Sistine Chapel (now become almost dark, the lights having been extinguished), and crossing the noble hall, called the Sala Regia, separating it from the Pauline Chapel, entered the latter, where on bended knees and in perfect silence, he venerated the Sacrament of the Eucharist, solemnly exposed to public adoration as already mentioned. This was one of the most magnificent sights of the Holy Week.

The Pauline Chapel was illuminated throughout from the roof to the pavement, with such a profusion of wax lights as to produce a degree of brilliancy that I do not remember to have before seen as the result of artificial means. The effect was beautiful, and being directed to a religious purpose, namely to honour Christ, believed by the worshippers to be present in the Host, what might otherwise appear as only a scenic display, became thus imbued with a spiritual meaning and object, which in the minds of Catholics present would connect a sentiment of religion with the physical illumination.

On Good Friday morning I heard the Mass of the Presanctified, as it is called, in the Sistine, celebrated pontifically by a cardinal before the Pope. From time immemorial no complete or perfect Mass has been celebrated on this day in the Roman Church. The officiating priest does indeed receive the communion, but no consecration of the eucharistic elements takes place to-day, they having been already consecrated at yesterday's Mass, and preserved during the interval in solemn state in a chapel handsomely decorated and set apart for the purpose, known by the name of The Sepulchre. In the case of the Sistine, the Pauline Chapel serves for its Sepulchre, as previously described. This Mass of the Presanctified is very peculiar, differing throughout from the ordinary service of the Mass. It commences with the clergy lying prostrate at the foot of the altar in silent prayer, as though the event to be commemorated was too awful to be expressed in words. Several Lessons are then read from the prophetical books of the Old Testament, referring to the coming of the Messiah, after which a series of prayers are intoned by the officiating cardinal, invoking the divine blessing on all mankind, without distinction of creed, heretics, Jews, and pagans being successively prayed for.

On the conclusion of these prayers the ancient ceremony of the Adoration of the Cross takes place, a ceremony peculiar to Good Friday, when a large crucifix being placed upon a cushion, the clergy and others reverently approach it, kneeling thrice whilst doing so, and then devoutly imprint a kiss on the image of the crucified Saviour. The Pope, cardinals, and clergy now went in procession to the Pauline Chapel to fetch the Host deposited there on the previous day. Upon their return, the Cardinal-celebrant said the concluding portion of the Mass, and received the communion. Vespers were afterwards recited by the choir, and the service was ended. The musical parts of the office of Good Friday morning, consisting entirely of chaunts, were most effectively performed by the papal choir; indeed, it is one of the best occasions for hearing the peculiar style of music for which this choir is famous.

In the afternoon of the same day, instead of hearing the Tenebræ Office for the third and last time at the Sistine, I repaired to the Conventual church of the Bambino Gesù, near Santa Maria Maggiore, where the same service was sweetly and impressively sung by the nuns of that monastery. The Lamentations of Jeremiah, and the Miserere, were beautifully performed to the melodious accompaniment of delicately played instruments. Of the small congregation present, the majority were ecclesiastics of various religious Orders.

On Holy Saturday, the grand service of the day is celebrated at the Basilica of St. John Lateran, by the Cardinal-vicar. I arrived before eight o'clock, but the office was already begun. It was exceedingly long, and continued without interruption till near two, including, (*inter alia*) a procession from the Basilica across the adjoining Piazza, to the Baptistery, where the annual ceremony of baptising converted Jews was performed by the Cardinal-vicar. The concluding portion of the service was interesting, from the fact that all the ecclesiastical orders were conferred upon a number of candidates, beginning with the lowest of the minor orders, and ending with that of priest.

On Easter Sunday I was among the first of the thousands who flocked to St. Peter's, to be present at the grand Pontifical High Mass celebrated by the Pope in person, and which was performed with an unrivalled splendour of ceremonial. The magnificence of this most splendid of ceremonies, whether of a religious or temporal character, renders any description of it a difficult task.

Whilst being carried in and out of the church in the chair of state, (the Sedia Gestatoria), the Pope wore the famous triple crown, or tiara, round which glittered three circles, one above the other, of brilliant jewels. Before the commencement of mass, he exchanged the tiara for the ordinary episcopal mitre. The cardinals present—twenty-six in number—wore on this occasion their mitres, and chasubles of white satin, embroidered with gold over red cassocks, with long trains, and surplices of the most elaborate lace. This was the first time I had seen the cardinals robed in their characteristic colour of red, for during Lent they use the penitential colour of purple. The *coup-d'œil* at the Elevation was strikingly beautiful, the grouping of the numerous dignitaries and officials, clothed in vestments suited to their rank and office, being arranged with great care and artistic skill at this crowning point of the service. The effect thus produced bears some resemblance to a *tableau-vivant*, and merits particular atten-

EASTER SUNDAY. 73

tion. On both to-day and Palm Sunday, there was a gorgeous effect of colouring, caused by the bright sun-beams falling on the coloured marbles of St. Peter's, as well as on the stately vestments of the assembled prelates, and the gay uniforms of the military men present. But these religious ceremonies, and especially the grand display on Easter Sunday, must be seen to be understood. They depend for their effect too much upon colour, form, and "pomp of circumstance," and on rich harmony of sound, to admit of being adequately described.

Nor would it be easy to give an idea of the appearance presented by the Piazza of St. Peter's, when the Pope, after the conclusion of high mass, having ascended to the balcony overlooking the main entrance to the Basilica, pronounced his apostolic benediction on the immense multitude assembled in the square beneath. This was really a fine sight. The enormous crowd of spectators, filling not only the Piazza, but every window commanding a view of it; the troops of different kinds, with their various uniforms, and weapons of burnished steel; the numerous handsome equipages, especially the state carriages of the cardinals; the tolling of the bells of St. Peter's; and, to crown the whole, a bright Italian sun, all concurred to produce a most striking spectacle. But more impressive still was the scene, when the Sovereign Pontiff wearing (if I remember right) the triple tiara, advanced to the front of the balcony, and with uplifted arms implored the blessing of Heaven upon the multitude below, while the assembled crowd received in silence and on bended knees the benediction thus pronounced. In a moment afterwards the booming of the guns of the Castle of St. Angelo sounded on the ear, mingled with the bells of the cathedral, and immediately the thousands who had filled the spacious Piazza, began quickly to disperse. As on the previous Sunday, the throng of pedestrians returning from St. Peter's, and the long line of cardinals' carriages, and those of other notabilities, was in itself an interesting sight.

In the evening of Easter day, the dome and west front of St. Peter's were illuminated, presenting the appearance, at a distance, of the whole church being lighted up. The effect of this illumination, as I beheld it from a tower of the Capuchin convent, was beautiful. If the exterior of St. Paul's were so illuminated, that the shape of the church should be distinctly discernible, and appear like a vast body of light that had taken that form, such would be the best description I could give of the illumination of St. Peter's. I was struck by the absence of glare, the quality of light produced being as soft and equal as that of a celestial body. All at once, on a given signal, the shade of light was skilfully made to change simultaneously throughout the edifice, and to become more brilliant than before, although still not glaringly so. The Romans are much interested by this change in the illumination, and watch eagerly for it, which I believe is caused by the simultaneous withdrawing of tiny paper bags, by which, until then, the myriads of lamps are covered. Much danger to the workmen employed is said to be attendant on this operation; and it is a current report, though I do not vouch for its truth, that the artificers engaged in these perilous portions of the work, receive the sacrament before undergoing the risk they involve. The illumination of St. Peter's is repeated on the 29th of June, St. Peter's day.

The celebration of Easter concluded on the evening of Easter Monday with a brilliant and very beautiful display of fireworks, called in Italian, " La Girandola," exhibited on the side of the Pincian hill, bordering on the Piazza del Popolo. The spectators stood in the Piazza, from which there was an excellent view of the fireworks on the rising ground of the Pincio. The Girandola was accompanied by salvos of artillery, both of which were intended to do honour to the festival of Easter.

CHAPTER IV.

The Churches of Rome.

THE churches of Italy, and especially those of Rome, suggest a very different order of ideas to the mind to those which are raised by the ecclesiastical edifices of England, France or Belgium—of Oxford, York and Salisbury, or of Rouen, Amiens and Antwerp.

York Minster and Westminster, Durham and Peterborough—the cathedrals of Amiens and Rouen, Mechlin and Tournay—seem eminently calculated, by their solemn grandeur of form, to excite sentiments of a serious and religious kind. The great churches of Italy, on the contrary, usually aim solely at producing the *beautiful*; they seldom rise to the grand or sublime except in the few Gothic exceptions

They are delightful galleries of art, including architecture, painting, sculpture, mosaics and every decorative accessory, such as gilding and colouring, &c., but the ideas and feelings they give rise to are rarely of that solemn and spiritual cast, so well known to the lovers of the Northern Gothic. In regard to the *exterior*, Italian churches are not generally imposing, and often not even pleasing to the eye. All the expense, skill, and artistic excellence are lavished on the decorations of the interior alone, to the serious detriment consequently of the external effect of the edifice. In many cases, the outsides of great and celebrated churches are left in an unfinished state, examples of which may be seen in the cathedral, and several of the finest churches of Florence, and in the Annunziata at Genoa; while, in others, although finished, the style of the exterior is altogether inferior to the architecture and decorations of the interior.

The consequence is that Italian churches do not generally constitute those majestic specimens of architecture to which we are accustomed in

Northern Europe. To say nothing of the exterior of St Peter's, to which I shall revert presently, how disappointing in external appearance is every one of the other great churches of Rome, with the solitary exception of St. John Lateran. How tame, externally, are Sta. Maria Maggiore, San Paolo fuori delle Mura, the Gesù and the other principal ecclesiastical edifices.* How different the effect produced on the beholder from that when he first comes in sight of Durham or Peterborough cathedrals, or of St. Ouen at Rouen, or St. Denis near Paris.

It is a remarkable fact that most of the churches in Italy, celebrated for fine exteriors— and the reader will bear in mind that at present I am speaking of exteriors only—are, either wholly or in part, of a style of architecture foreign to the ordinary Italian styles. Thus the superb exterior of Milan cathedral is Gothic,

* It is true that several of the Roman churches possess fine domes, which doubtless have a grand and imposing effect; but even in these instances the otherwise tame and unimpressive character of the external architecture is by no means compensated for.

the beautiful exterior of St. Mark's at Venice is Byzantine, the fine exterior of the cathedral of Pisa is Greco-Arabian, and the handsome front of the cathedral of Sienna is Gothic. The Duomo at Florence, too, which in spite of the unfinished façade, is imposing, is Tuscan Gothic. But if it be true of the cathedrals, that their external appearance generally bears no proportion to the interior, this is still more true in regard to the second-rate churches in Italy; and yet the expense, labour, and high artistic skill lavished on the interiors of Italian churches, not only of the larger edifices, but also on second, third, and even fourth-rate churches would be scarcely credible to any one who had not seen them. Many a church in every part of Italy containing much that is beautiful and worthy of examination, is passed by unheeded by travellers who expect to find in the exterior of an Italian church some indication of its claims to attention within.

I venture to think that even St. Peter's itself cannot be altogether excepted from the foregoing remarks. The dome, indeed, is not only beautiful, but very grand; the semicircular colonnades with their forest of columns stretching out on either side from the front of the church, and enclosing a sort of open court before it, are exceedingly elegant, and the spacious flight of marble steps leading up to the church is most handsome. But the façade itself, with its rows of square English-looking windows, suggests to the mind the front of some great palace, or hotel-de-ville, rather than of the largest and most celebrated ecclesiastical edifice in the world. It must however be remembered that Michael Angelo planned a totally different façade to the existing one, but as his death occurred during the progress of the building, the present front was substituted by his successors in the work. Whatever may be thought of the exterior effect of St. Peter's, it is impossible to feel otherwise than delighted and amazed with the splendid result of human genius and perseverance exhibited in the interior of the Vatican Basilica. It is undoubtedly a grand and impressive spectacle that presents itself to the view, when, after pushing aside the ponderous curtain separating the inside of the church from the spacious and beautiful vestibule, you stand at the entrance of the nave.

The first impression of most travellers is that the building is much less extensive than it really is, but as they proceed in their examination of the church, and especially after several visits, they gradually realize the immense extent of space comprised within its walls—the height and breadth of the nave and aisles, the extreme beauty of the sculpture, mosaics, frescoes, and other paintings, the profusion of marbles by which the edifice is incrusted, independent of the marble columns, and handsome pavement of the same material—and, in a word, the mind, after a time, begins to form a full conception of the gigantic whole, that constitutes the matchless grandeur and elegance of St. Peter's.

I shall not easily forget the impression derived from my first visit to this splendid church. I was accompanied by a friar of the convent where I was staying, and as we ascended the magnificent flight of marble steps leading up to the church, my companion exclaimed, " Behold the

cause of the Reformation!" alluding of course
to the sale of indulgences, for the purpose of
obtaining the funds necessary for completing the
new Basilica, which so justly scandalized the
early Reformers. I was a little surprised to
hear such a remark from a Catholic and a priest,
and yet this was a most zealous and devout
young friar, only recently ordained, and much
respected in his Order.

As I entered, and obtained my first view of
the majestic nave, and the Shrine of the Apostles
at the upper end, with a hundred gilt lamps
burning before it, I heard distant tones of an
organ, and the effect thus produced upon the
sense of hearing, combined with that on the
sense of sight, to which was added the influence
of the imagination, which could scarcely fail to
be excited by the thought of making one's first
visit to St. Peter's, was impressive to a degree
it would be difficult to describe, and each suc-
ceeding visit increased my feeling of that grandeur and beauty by which I was so much struck
on the first occasion. To complete my knowledge of this splendid temple, I mounted to the

extreme top of the ball over the dome, before I quitted Rome, and was amply repaid for the exertion by the strong relief in which the immense extent and height of the building was presented to the view, as well as by the fine prospect it afforded over Rome and the surrounding country. It also enabled me to realize more fully than I had ever done before the prodigious space of ground occupied by the successive quadrangles of the Vatican Palace, which adjoins the Basilica.

Besides St. Peter's, Rome possesses numerous fine churches, many of them enriched with beautiful art treasures, in the shape of pictures, frescoes, and sculpture. The limits of this volume preclude any attempt to enter upon so wide a field as a detailed account of the churches of Rome, so that I must content myself with a passing notice of a few of the principal of them.

Among these is St. John Lateran, which ranks first of the seven Patriarchal churches of Rome, and takes precedence of all other churches in the world. It is said to have been originally erected by Constantine, but the present building appears to be comparatively modern. It is a spacious, handsome, and stately church, and has the somewhat rare merit in Italy of a fine exterior. The Cloister* adjoining the Basilica is exceedingly elegant. Attached to the church is the Lateran Palace, where Innocent III, in 1215, held the great Œcumenical Council known by the name of the Fourth Council of Lateran. The other six Patriarchal Basilicas are St. Peter's, Sta. Maria Maggiore, Sta. Croce in Gerusalemme, San Paolo fuori delle Mura, San Lorenzo, and San Sebastiano, of which we

* I was glad subsequently to find my judgment on objects of Italian art, confirmed in two instances by that of the constructors of the "Italian Court," in the Crystal Palace. These two instances are the Certosa of Pavia (see Chap. XIV), from which more objects of art have been copied in the "Italian Court," than from any other building in Italy; and the beautiful cloister of St. John Lateran, a section from which—notwithstanding its having been pronounced by an English authoress of reputation to be "in the very vilest style of architecture"—has been selected (as I think, with much discrimination) by the same authorities as a type of Italian claustral architecture.

will say a few words in succession, and then proceed to notice briefly some of the remaining principal churches in Rome.

Sta. Maria Maggiore forms quite a museum of paintings, sculpture, mosaics, marbles, and other artistic decorations. This church seems to me to give a truer idea of an ancient Basilica than any other building I know; the immense oblong nave, supported by forty antique Ionic columns, with a perfectly flat Renaissance roof, producing a thoroughly classical effect, which is not diminished by the rectangular and formal aspect of the whole edifice. The Borghese chapel in this church was built by Paul V, and is celebrated for the magnificence of its decorations. Sta. Croce in Gerusalemme is the church of the Cistercian monastery, to which it is contiguous; but although handsome it cannot be called remarkable among the many larger and finer churches in Rome. It is, as already stated, one of the seven Patriarchal Basilicas, and one also of the four—St. Peter's, St. John Lateran, Sta. Maria Maggiore, and Sta. Croce—which stand within Rome itself, the three others, San

Paolo, San Lorenzo, and San Sebastiano, being at some distance beyond the walls.

The old Basilica of San Paolo fuori delle Mura, distant about four or five miles from the centre of Rome, and built by Constantine, was destroyed by fire upwards of thirty years ago. It is described as having been a most venerable and stately edifice. The nave and aisles were supported by eighty ancient columns, and the altars by thirty columns of porphyry; and above the columns of the nave were placed portraits of all the Popes, two hundred and fifty in number, from St. Peter to Pius VII. It redounds greatly to the credit of the Papal government, that although so short a time has elapsed since the destruction of the ancient Basilica, and although even that short period has been marked by serious political disturbances, a new church has already arisen on the ruins of the old, which for size and elegance is perhaps unsurpassed by any modern ecclesiastical edifice. I speak only of the interior, for the exterior more resembles a gigantic Methodist chapel, than a building which internally can vie with any church that has been built during the present century. From this criticism on the exterior of the church, must however be excepted the elegant portico forming the entrance to the northern transept, nor was the west front finished at the period of my visit. The whole series of portraits of the Popes are being carefully restored in mosaic, involving of course an enormous outlay of money and labour.

San Paolo fuori delle Mura, is the church of the great Benedictine Abbey attached to it. The abbey itself was happily uninjured by the fire, and contains a very beautiful cloister, around which are written some curious old Latin verses, which I regret having omitted to copy. Much as I admire the exquisite Gothic cloisters of England, I think some of those in Italy, in the Italian style, are equal to them in beautiful effect. The cloisters of San Paolo, St. John Lateran, Sta. Maria degli Angeli, those at San Martino at Naples, and above all those of the Carthusian Priory, near Pavia, are admirable specimens of claustral architecture. The Abbot of San Paolo is not only mitred, but exercises episcopal jurisdiction over a considerable space of country surrounding the abbey. Previous to the Reformation, the kings of England had the title of Protector of this Basilica. The monks have another monastery in Rome itself, called San Callisto, where they reside between May and November, on account of the unhealthiness of the Campagna in the hot season. During the period of their residence at San Callisto, some of the monks are conveyed daily in carriages to San Paolo to perform the ordinary services there.

San Lorenzo, another of the Seven Patriarchal Basilicas, and standing like the preceding in the Campagna, is in point of its internal architecture a strikingly elegant church, at least so far as regards the choir, which forms part of what, anterior to the time of Constantine, was a Temple of Neptune. The nave is ascribed to that emperor; it is evidently of later date than the choir, and greatly inferior to it. Beneath the church are catacombs, a very small part only of which has been excavated. The monastery attached to San Lorenzo is tenanted by Capuchin Friars. I visited it and the church in company with a friar of the convent at Rome, where I was a visitor. I was amused by the laconic but expressive way in which he introduced me to the Superior of San Lorenzo. "Ecco un Signore Inglese," he said, "Non è Catolico, ma non ha prejudicj."* The Superior ordered coffee to be brought to his cell, where we were. He was a Swiss, and filled at the same time the office of parish priest, San Lorenzo being a parochial church. As has been before observed, it is far from uncommon in Italy for conventual churches to be parochial, in which case some one of the monks or friars is appointed the "parroco," or rector.

The last of the Patriarchal Basilicas, is San Sebastiano, about two miles beyond the gate of the same name, and double that distance from Rome, whose gates are in many instances far removed from the modern town, on account of the latter occupying much less ground than the

* "Here is an English gentleman. He is not a Catholic, but he has no prejudices."

ancient city. San Sebastiano is a spacious and handsome Basilica-shaped church, but is mainly remarkable for the catacombs beneath it, which are of considerable size and highly interesting. They will not however bear comparison with the celebrated catacombs of San Callisto, on the same road as San Sebastiano, between it and Rome. Persons desirous of obtaining an adequate idea of the extent of the catacombs and of the great amount of archæological information which their paintings and inscriptions afford, should endeavour to visit the catacombs of San Callisto, in company with some one who has made the subject his study. I had the advantage of visiting San Callisto under the guidance of the Rev. Mr. Northcote, who has since published a work on the Roman Catacombs.

Among the other principal churches of Rome are the Pantheon, which was converted at an early period from a Pagan to a Christian church;[*] the Gesù, or church of the Jesuits;

[*] The Pantheon is believed to have been built by Agrippa, son-in-law of Augustus, and to have been dedicated in honour of all the gods, although Palladius

the church of the Twelve Apostles, founded by Constantine; the Basilica of St. Mark, behind the Piazza di Venezia, to which you descend by

supposed the body of the building, that is the circular portion, to have been erected during the Republic. On the frieze may yet be read the following inscription:—

M. Agrippa. L. F. Cos. Tertium
Fecit.

The Pantheon is in form a rotunda, with a Greek façade or portico. To the spectator standing in the picturesque Piazza, of which the Pantheon forms one side, this stately edifice recalls vividly the times in which it was built, so thoroughly and grandly expressive of great age is this venerable relic of antiquity. Often as I have passed during the course of two visits to Rome, across the Piazza della Rotunda—for so is this square now called—I could never cast even a cursory glance at the Pantheon, without feeling as if a living bit of ancient Rome had arisen from the tomb of Time. The complete state of preservation of this building, the original inscription being still distinctly legible on its façade, adds to this feeling. For in the Pantheon you do not see a ruin such as the Coliseum, the remains of the Forum, the Temple of Peace, and most other monuments of Imperial Rome, but a well preserved temple, which (the impress of age excepted) must have appeared the same in the reign of Augustus, as it does in a flight of steps, the pavement of the church being below the surrounding level; San Carlo al Corso, a stately edifice with a fine dome, forming a prominent object from the Pincio, and most of the eminences from which travellers obtain views of Rome; Sta. Maria degli Angeli, the Carthusian church, of great extent and ancient form, having been the great Hall of Diocletian's Baths, out of which latter the adjoining Carthusian monastery has been constructed; and San Pietro in Vincolo, where is Michael Angelo's famous statue of Moses.

The Dominican church of Sta. Maria sopra Minerva, is remarkable for being the only Gothic church in Rome, so little does Gothic architecture appear to flourish there, and the exterior of even this solitary specimen of Roman Gothic, is a mere square whitewashed building,

that of Pius IX. If the Arch of Titus may be considered as an historical memorial of the taking of Jerusalem, and of the dispersion of the Jews, the Pantheon may be regarded as a memorial at least contemporary with the foundation of the Roman Empire in the person of Augustus.

after the manner of a Dissenting chapel in England, previous to the recent improvements in the style of ecclesiastical architecture among many of the English Dissenting bodies. This church contains a fine statue of Christ by Michael Angelo.* In the Piazza, which takes its name from the church of the Minerva, is the ecclesiastical College of the Accademia, the students in which are generally persons designed to fill the higher offices in the church. The church of Sta. Maria della Pace, beyond the Piazza Navona, is enriched by possessing the treasure of Raphael's Fresco of the Sybils, which is thought by many to be that master's greatest work in point of composition.

* Another Gothic church was in course of construction when I was at Rome, intended for the Redemptorist Fathers. It stands near Sta. Maria Maggiore, on the road leading thence to St. John Lateran. The chapel of the nuns of I Sacri Cuori, in Transtevere, is a pleasing specimen of Gothic, but is not, I believe, open to the public.

CHAPTER V.

Monastic Life at Rome.

THE reader of Andersen's "Improvisatore," may remember the sketch of a monastery given in the opening pages of that vivid picture of Italian life. Andersen speaks of "the convent "where the open colonnade, which enclosed "within a square the little potato garden, with "the two cypress and orange-trees, made a very "deep impression upon me. Side by side, in the "open passages, hung old portraits of deceased "monks, and on the door of each cell were posted "pictures from the history of the martyrs, which "I contemplated with the same holy emotion as "afterwards the master-pieces of Raphael, and "Andrea del Sarto."

It was in this same convent that I was now to tarry awhile as a visitor, although as already stated, it was not without difficulty (in spite of an excellent introduction) that I prevailed on the Superior to receive me, so contrary is it to the usual practice of Italian monasteries to admit visitors for however limited a period.

The Convent of Santa Maria della Concezione, or as it is more often called, La Concezione only, was built two centuries and a half ago, by Cardinal Francesco Barberini, brother of Urban VIII. It belongs to the Order of Capuchins, who constitute one of the several reformations, or branches, into which the Franciscans are divided. They are Mendicants, earning their scanty subsistence by begging alms, either in kind or in money. But while they live on the voluntary contributions of the people, they are among the most liberal of the religious Orders in exercising charity to the poor; and this, together with the known rigidity of the life they lead, causes them to be held in very general estimation. The costume worn by the Capuchins consists of a coarse brown cloth habit, or cassock, extending to the ankles, over which they have a short cloak of the same material and colour. On the head they wear a small skull-cap, and in cold or wet weather, a cowl drawn over the head, but at other times this is allowed to hang behind the neck unused, resembling the hood of a lady's mantle. Leather sandles form the only protection for their feet; and from the waist hangs on one side a rosary of large wooden beads, and from the other a thick cord with three knots in it at intervals, intended as symbols of the three principal monastic vows.

Like all convents of the Capuchin Order, and indeed of most of the Mendicant Orders, the Convent of La Concezione is built on a plan of studied simplicity, in accordance with the humility and the poverty professed by the disciples of St. Francis. But although without architectural pretensions, the convent is very large, containing an immense number of cells, and extending over a considerable space of ground. It comprises no less than four quadrangles of buildings, two of which have the usual conventual cloisters running round them. There are upwards of six hundred cells, as I was informed, the majority of which are intended for the accommodation of the deputies from each Capuchin convent in the world, who resort to Rome on the occasion of the General Chapter of the Order, held once in six years.

I was given to understand that on these occasions the cells are not only all filled, but that a portion of the "Family" of the convent—that is, the regular resident community of monks or friars, belonging to a particular monastery—have to be draughted off to other convents, in order that more room may be rendered available for the deputies from foreign countries.

The convent-gate opens into a large cloister, or open quadrangular space enclosed by a covered walk extending round its four sides. Over the gateway are placed the arms of the Franciscan Order, and also those of the Cardinal-Protector of the Capuchins, several of the religious bodies having a special patron among the College of Cardinals, who is styled their Protector. The threshold of the convent-gate marks the "Clausura," or limit beyond which women are forbidden to pass.

In illustration of the severity with which the "Clausura," or monastic enclosure, is enforced in Italy in convents of men, I may mention that an English lady told me that happening to be walking in the neighbourhood of Pisa in the spring of 1859, she saw the gate of a monastery open, and a handsome cloister within. Wishing to see the cloister more thoroughly, and quite unaware that she was doing anything wrong, she stepped inside the doorway. Many moments had not elapsed before a white-robed lay-brother of powerful frame emerged unexpectedly from the conventual buildings, and with the rapidity of lightning, taking her by the shoulders, forced her out of the cloister, loading her at the same time with reproaches for her unintentional intrusion.

I saw a similar occurrence myself in the Convent of La Concezione. The gateway is often besieged by beggars and others of both sexes,

waiting the arrival of some of the friars. The
men are allowed to enter the cloister, but
women are strictly required to remain without.
On one occasion, when I was walking in the
cloister, an Italian woman, thinking, it would
seem, that enough attention was not paid to
her, stepped a foot or two inside the doorway,
and seemed to be looking round for some one
to speak to. No sooner, however, had she
done so, than two of the porters (of whom, at
this large monastery there are three) rushed
from their lodge, and seizing her, one by one
shoulder, and the other by the other, sum-
marily ejected her from the claustral precincts.
Probably, in both instances, the porters of the
respective convents acted thus peremptorily from
a conviction that they would be held responsible
for the slightest infraction of the monastic enclosure, which in Italy is looked upon as in-
violable by any woman worthy of respect. Had
the same persons been in the conventual church
when it was desired to clear it of strangers, they
would have been politely requested to leave;
but for infringing the enclosure, however

slightly, it was apparently deemed necessary to administer a pretty sharp rebuke.

The walls of the principal cloister are decorated with fairly-executed portraits of notabilities of the Capuchin Order, already alluded to in the extract quoted above from the "Improvisatore." The second cloister which is connected with the former by a short passage, contains a rough but bright-coloured fresco of the Madonna, together with a fountain, always playing, and a beautiful painting of the Virgin over an altar in a corner of the cloister. It is said that the Pope—or some pope, for I do not remember which—esteemed this picture so highly, that he threatened to have it removed elsewhere, unless the friars took more care of it than it would appear to have received formerly. It represents the "Madonna Addolorata," the Woman of Sorrows; but while the expression is eminently sorrowful, there is mingled with the sorrow, a sweet hopeful tenderness, that is very charming. Each of the quadrangles formed by these cloisters contains a flower-garden; the flowers in the first cloister being

intended, as I was told, "per bellezza," for
beauty; and those in the other, for decorating
the altars of the convent-church.

From the cloisters you ascend by a staircase
to the dormitories. On this stair-case is an
altar dedicated to the Virgin, with a pretty
painting representing her. The altar itself, like
every altar of the Roman Catholic Church, has
for its centre and chief ornament, an image of
the Crucified Saviour. The dormitories, as
previously explained, are the corridors or passages into which the cells of the friars open.
The number of the dormitories in this convent
is in proportion to its great size. They contain
several chapels and altars for the private devotions of the monastic inmates, and a few large
crucifixes placed here and there against the
walls. There are also curious as well as interesting statistical tables of the Order posted up
in the dormitories, showing the total number of
its members, and the proportion of these in
every country, also the number of convents,
and a variety of other details, thus admitting
the reader to an intimate and authentic know-

ledge of the statistics of one of the most numerous religious Orders existing.

The cells have each a woodcut of some saint on the outside of the door, and their furniture usually comprises a little bed, a crucifix, a *bénêtier*, and several prints of saints. Their dimensions may perhaps be ten feet long by about six wide, and instead of glass they have linen windows. The floors are of brick. The Capuchins use no sheets but only blankets for bed-clothes, and they sleep in their monastic habit. The dormitories are on the first and second stories, extending round the quadrangles formed by the several cloisters, with cells along both sides of the corridors, so that the windows of the cells on one side of the dormitories look into a cloister, and those on the opposite side open either into another cloister, or the spacious gardens belonging to the convent. The cells, one of which is appropriated to each friar, are used by them for sleeping, and also throughout the day for study, writing, and so forth. Indeed when a monk or friar is not in church, or the refectory, or engaged on some business connected with his monastery, he is supposed to be, and is in fact, generally to be found in his cell.

The refectory of the convent I am describing is unusually large, although scarcely spacious enough to accommodate the numerous community who live there. It consists of an oblong chamber or hall, with a folding door at the lower end, and long narrow tables of polished oak, along the two sides and upper end. The benches forming the seats for the friars are here placed along both sides of the tables, and there is even a third row of tables in the middle of the refectory. But in most refectories, when the community is only moderately numerous, the seats are on the inner side alone, next the wall, the outer side of the tables, as well as the centre of the room, being thus left unoccupied. The lay-brothers carry in the dishes, or rather each person's allotted portion ready served out on a plate, upon large wooden trays, with spaces scooped out in them of a form and size capable of receiving a plate each. These trays are carried by the lay-brothers on their shoulders, and hold from about one to two dozen portions.

The friars repair to the refectory twice a day, at a quarter past eleven in the morning for dinner, or at noon if it be Lent; and at the Ave Maria, or hour of sun-set, for supper. They are summoned to their frugal repast by a sound produced by striking an iron bar against a great piece of stone or metal suspended from a wall. The noise thus caused is sufficiently harsh, but very effectual, reverberating as it does through every part of the convent. The brotherhood stand in two rows in the middle of the refectory whilst grace is said, and the effect of the responses, taken up in unison by so large a body of friars, is impressive. Grace being concluded, and all having taken their respective seats, each friar opens a drawer in the table containing his own napkin, knife and fork, and spoon, and spreads the napkin upon the table in front of him by way of table-cloth. This having been done, he begins his slender meal. A Capuchin dinner usually consists of "minestra," or soup, a very small portion of meat, and a plate of vegetables. Supper comprises a thin soup, and a tiny piece of meat. On fast days, of course, they take no meat; nor do they have supper on those days, but "colezione," or collation only, consisting of some boiled vegetable and a smaller allowance of bread than usual. Their drink is wine and water, ready mixed. During meals complete silence is observed, and one of the junior friars, (or several in succession) reads in a loud voice from a devotional book for the general edification.

When the meal is ended, the whole community rises, on a sign being given by the Superior, and forming as before in two lines along the centre of the refectory, a thanksgiving is recited, with responses, as mentioned above. It may be here observed that in Italian convents generally, no regular breakfast is served, but only a cup of "caffè nero," or coffee without milk, and a mouthful of dry bread. This is not taken in the refectory, but in a chamber set apart for the purpose, where each friar takes his cup of coffee and morsel of bread soaked in it, at any time that suits him from about seven o'clock to nine. In the whole matter of diet, the religious communities with which I am acquainted are most abstemious; and were it not that Italians seem to require so little food compared with the inhabitants of more northern climates, it would often appear surprising how the friars contrive to subsist on so small a quantity of nourishment.

The religious community of the convent of La Concezione may be divided into three divisions, first, the " Famiglia," or Family, that is to say, the friars appertaining to the convent; secondly, the sick and infirm in the Infirmary, for this being the chief house, ("casa provinciale") of the Province of Rome, it has as usual the provincial hospital; and lastly, a certain number of " birds of passage," or Capuchins who have come from various parts of the world to Rome on ecclesiastical business, and who reside in the convent during their stay there. At the period of my visit, the total number of Religious within the walls was about one hundred and eighty. The " Famiglia," or Family, consisted, I believe, of one hundred and twenty, or thereabouts, the remainder being divided between the other two classes just mentioned, viz., the inmates of the provincial infirmary, and the strangers whom casual business connected with the Order had brought to Rome.

From the Family strictly so called, however, should be deducted the various officials connected with the general government of the Capuchin Order throughout the world, this being the head-house of the whole Order, and as such, the residence of the General and his staff; likewise some thirteen students of Elocution, all of them professed friars, and in priests' orders, who were completing their clerical education by devoting twelve months to a special preparation for the pulpit. These deductions would probably reduce the number of the regular community of the convent by about forty persons.

The friars, and the inmates of religious houses generally, (as has been mentioned in describing the Barnabite Convent at Genoa) are divided into two bodies; those in holy orders, styled "Padri," and those who have taken the vows and are regularly professed, but have not received clerical orders, and these are called "Laici," or lay-brothers. The Padri serve the community spiritually, by saying mass, singing the seven Canonical Hours of Prayer, preaching, hearing confessions, &c.; while the lay-brothers attend to the temporal affairs of the convent, such as cooking, serving at table, cultivating the garden, begging alms, &c.

The Padri, or priests, pass through a long period of study to prepare them for the priesthood, and are therefore usually well instructed in their own particular branches of study, especially in Latin and in dogmatic theology; and among their number in each convent are commonly to be found some men of varied reading and general information. The lay-brothers, on the other hand, do not profess to be literate, although they are often models of the ascetic virtues. To render complete this statement of the divisions or classes into which the inmates of a religious house are divided, it should be mentioned that there is frequently a third body, called Clerks, or in Italian, "Chierici."

When a monk or friar, after passing the twelve months novitiate, takes the monastic vows, he is said to be *professed*. At a person's profession he either undertakes to serve the community as a lay-brother, or else proceeds to prepare himself for holy orders, in which latter case he enters on a course of study extending over several years. During this period of study, his *status* is that of a Clerk, or "Chierico." No mention is here made of the Novices, who form a fourth estate of the monastic society, because one convent only in each Province of a religious Order receives novices, whence it is known by the name of the "Noviziato," or Novitiate House. Thus, excepting this single convent in every province, novices do not generally constitute a part of the inmates of a monastery. This rule of one Novitiate House only to each province, is common to all Orders with which I am acquainted.

The ordinary daily routine at the Capuchin Convent at Rome commenced at midnight, the friars being aroused by a sort of rattle made of wood and iron (in Italian " troccolo") which is sounded through the dormitories, and so effectual are these for the purpose that the hardest sleeper is sure to be awakened. I have heard that wakeful persons in the houses of the adjoining Piazza can often hear these midnight rattles, although of course they are only used within the walls. The church bell is rung in addition, so that the reader will not be surprised to hear that, being unable to sleep through the night, even had I wished, I frequently rose to be present at the chaunting in choir of Matins at midnight.[*] The picturesque effect of this unusual sight, and the mediæval associations suggested by it, may easily be conceived. In a large choir lighted by a single oil lamp, just enough to make "darkness visible," stood the quaint-looking friars chaunting in a deep bass voice the psalms, hymns, and responses of the

[*] The ancient practice of singing Matins at midnight, is founded on the 119th Psalm, verse 62, "At midnight I will rise to give thanks unto thee: because of thy righteous judgments."

Roman Liturgy. Their uniform chaunt was occasionally broken by the solitary voice of the officiating priest, reading the collects and lessons of the day. It was impressive to hear the Te Deum at the end of Matins sung at this solemn hour of the night, accompanied by the tolling of the church bell, as is customary in convents when the Ambrosian Hymn is recited. The dormitories are kept lighted throughout the night, so that you may go to Matins, even from a distant part of the building, without carrying a lamp. When the midnight office is ended, all return to their cells in silence.

The choir of the Capuchin Church, with the assembled friars singing their office, forms the subject of a coloured engraving commonly exhibited for sale in the picture shops of Rome. It is behind the high altar, and walled off from the nave. When in choir, the friars stand towards the altar with their faces turned consequently towards the people, (much as the congregation in the chancel of an English church are face to face with those in the nave) although concealed from their view by the walled partition. In the middle of the choir is a lectern with a large 'Chorale' upon it, containing the psalter and hymns used in divine service. The friars habitually sing the psalms and hymns of the Breviary from memory, without reference to a book, but the pages of the Chorale are kept duly turned for the benefit of any one whose memory may be at fault. By day, indeed, any friar thus situated often refers to a pocket prayer book, but at matins this resource is rendered unavailable by want of light, the choir being lit only by a solitary oil lamp over the lectern.

The pages of the Chorale are turned by a "chierico" or clerk, (that is a young professed friar, studying for holy orders) by means of a piece of wood resembling a large paper-knife, perhaps a foot and a half long by an inch wide, made for the purpose, with which he is easily enabled to reach the huge book on its elevated stand. These Chorales are printed on parchment, and the type is so large (each letter of one that I measured being only just covered by my thumb nail when laid upon it) that they may be read from a distance without the necessity of going close to the book. The object of this becomes apparent when, as occasionally happens, some exceptional psalm or hymn is sung, in which case I have seen nearly the whole community leave their places and approach within reading distance of the Chorale for reference.

The officiating clergyman at the Canonical Hours (who is styled "Hebdomadar" because the office is held for a week only at a time) stands in the centre of the choir near the east end, a little behind the lectern. But on great festivals, at matins and vespers, the Hebdomadar of the week vacates his office *pro hâc vice*, in favour of the senior dignitary of the friars present. The ninth or concluding lesson at matins moreover is always read by the senior dignitary, who for this purpose divests himself of his "mantello" or short monastic cloak, which is also invariably done by the Hebdomadar before commencing service.

For matins and vespers the church bell is tolled thrice; for the other hours, only twice.

RITUAL CEREMONIES. 115

The senior friar gives the signal for beginning the last bell by a tap with his hand, and by another tap he signifies that the service is to commence, whereupon all rise and the officiant intones the words, "Deus in adjutorium meum intende," to which the choir respond, "Et ad adjuvandum me festina." The doxology immediately follows, during which the friars turn to the right or left as the case may be, so as to face one another, at the same time bowing the head towards the ground in token of reverence for the Trinity.

As soon as the doxology is concluded, they resume their former position towards the altar. The Canonical Hours of the Breviary nearly all commence in the same way, and they consist for the most part of psalms interspersed with a few hymns, collects and responses, to which are added, in the case of matins, a series of lessons, generally nine in number, although on minor festivals there are but three. The office of matins is divided into nocturns,* each

* In the preface to the Book of Common Prayer several parts of the Breviary, and especially of matins,

series of three lessons with their appointed psalms &c., constituting one nocturn.

At six in the morning, the friars having taken

"A hasty portion of prescribed sleep;
Obedient slumbers that can wake and weep,
And sing, and sigh, and work, and sleep again,"*

---

are referred to by name as having been in use in the Church of England before the Reformation. In referring to the unreformed, or Roman Liturgy, which for a long series of centuries formed the common prayer of the English nation, the Prayer Book makes particular mention of nocturns, and of "anthems, responds, invitatories, and such like things," all which are portions of the Liturgy used to this day by the Roman Church. There was an archæological interest in hearing the same services read or sung at the present day, which were so familiar to our forefathers, as (independently of historical evidence) is shewn, not only by the preface to the Prayer Book, but also by the English Liturgy itself being, to a considerable extent, based upon the Roman Breviary, which is sufficiently apparent on a comparison of the two.—See the antiquities of the English ritual critically examined in the "Origines Liturgicæ," by the Rev. William Palmer, M.A., Fourth Edition, London: 1845.

* Crashaw.

were again summoned to choir by sound of bell, there to hear two masses, immediately after which the Canonical Hours called Prime and Tierce, or Terce, were sung. The subject of silent meditation in choir, forming as it does, an essential part of monastic discipline as it exists in Italy, has been slightly touched upon in a preceding chapter. The practice of the community assembling at a fixed hour, both morning and evening, in the choir of the church, and there devoting an allotted space of time, generally about half an hour, to silent communion with themselves, or meditation, is one of the most impressive phases of conventual life. This custom alone seemed to make a marked distinction between living in a monastery or in the busy world. People engaged in the active duties of life seldom have the opportunity, even when there is the inclination, to make a habit of regular meditation—of daily self-communion at fixed hours and for a definite time, in whatever circumstances they may happen to be placed.

Among the Capuchins, the impressiveness of

this part of the devotional exercises of the day is increased by the meditation always taking place with the window-shutters or blinds closed, thus excluding the light of day (for even the evening meditation being about the hour of sunset, would otherwise be by daylight), with the intention doubtless of giving a serious hue to the train of thought, and by withdrawing sensible objects from the view, to lead the mind to concentrate itself more entirely on the interior state of the soul.

At a quarter before eleven the friars again went into choir to sing Sext and None,* which are the third and fourth of the seven parts into which the Breviary, or the common prayer of the Roman Church, is divided.

From the choir the brotherhood repaired at once to the refectory for dinner. Some account of conventual meals, and the forms connected with them, having been already given, it will

---

* The office of the Breviary is divided into seven parts, called the Canonical Hours. These seven parts are matins and lauds, prime, tierce, sext, none, vespers, and complin.

be unnecessary to describe them again here. After dinner the friars spent a short time in recreation in the refectory or garden; or now and then a knot of friends would gather together in some favourite nook of this extensive monastery, and pass away half an hour in familiar conversation. Next followed a couple of hours of silence, during which the brotherhood remained in their respective cells. In the afternoon, varying according to the season of the year from one to about three, vespers were sung in choir. At a later hour, (precisely one hour and a quarter before the "Ave Maria," or sunset) complin was chaunted, followed by the Litany of the Madonna, and the reading of a chapter from some devotional book. The office terminated with the silent meditation previously described. Supper was then served in the refectory, whence they again proceeded to choir, where after a few prayers, the Superior blessed all present with holy water, as mentioned in the account of the Barnabite Convent at Genoa. This concluded the day's routine.

But although much time is occupied by these

often-recurring religious exercises. the intervals appeared to be turned to good account. The lay-brothers were actively employed in cultivating the extensive garden-land, or in cooking, serving at table, and other household occupations, besides begging alms for the community, and working in one or other of the several factories attached to the convent, which will be mentioned presently. Many secular labourers were retained in their service by the friars to assist in some of these duties, especially in cultivating the gardens, and in the cloth factory. The ordinary employments of the Padri, (or such as are in holy orders) are celebrating mass each morning, and reciting the seven Canonical Hours of the Breviary daily ; and, when occasion requires, hearing confessions, preaching, &c. Some of them, moreover, spend a good deal of time in study. Over and above these ordinary duties, the friars at Rome have the additional function of attending funerals, for which they receive an alms. It is the practice to have to most funerals an " accompanimento," or accompaniment of friars, who carry lighted wax candles, and chaunt psalms for the repose of the soul of the deceased, in proportion to whose station in life is the number of friars in attendance. A considerable body of the Capuchins are appointed daily to this duty, which is usually performed in the afternoon. These funerals, with their long trains of chaunting friars, often including those of several Orders at one funeral, are among the characteristics of Papal Rome.

The convent church, although approached by a handsome flight of steps, is like most churches of this Order, simple in style, and unpretentious in point of decoration. It is however, rich in paintings. The picture in the chapel on the right, is a St. Michael, by Guido, and enjoys a high celebrity, being considered by some to be that master's finest easel painting. It exhibits the Archangel contending with, or rather in the act of vanquishing, Satan; and its peculiar excellence consists in the admirable blending in one person of superhuman size and strength, with an angelic beauty of countenance and form. The fresco over the church door is by Giotto, and has been copied in mosaic in the portico of St. Peter's. There is also in St. Peter's a mosaic of Guido's St. Michael, but the copy is very inferior to the original. A third painting of note in the Capuchin church, is that of St. Paul receiving his sight, by Pietro da Cortona.

The catacombs beneath this church are celebrated for the curious exhibition they display of human bones formed into various fanciful designs, and fastened to the walls as a sort of grim decoration; while numerous corpses of friars in their monastic habit, are placed in an erect position, looking ghastly enough. Andersen, in the work quoted at the beginning of this chapter, speaking of this strange spectacle, makes his hero in his childhood say:

"We descended, and now I saw round about "me skulls upon skulls, so placed one upon "another, that they formed walls, and therewith "several chapels. In these were regular niches, "in which were seated perfect skeletons of the "most distinguished of the monks, enveloped in "their brown cowls, their cords round their

"waists, and with a breviary or a withered bunch
" of flowers in their hands. Altars, chandeliers,
" and ornaments were made of shoulder-bones
" and vertebræ, with bas-reliefs of human joints,
" horrible and tasteless as the whole idea. I
" clung fast to the monk, who whispered a prayer,
" and then said to me, ' Here also shall I some
" time sleep; wilt thou thus visit me?'
"I answered not a word, but looked horrified
" at him, and then round about me upon the
" strange grisly assembly. It was foolish to take
" me, a child, into this place. I was singularly
" impressed by the whole thing, and did not find
" myself again easy until I came into his little
" cell, where the beautiful yellow oranges almost
" hung in at the window, and I saw the brightly-
" coloured picture of the Madonna, who was
" borne upwards by angels into the clear sun-
" shine, while a thousand flowers filled the grave
" in which she had rested."

Mass was frequently said in these catacombs, and on every Monday* night they were lighted

* In the Roman Catholic Church, Monday is regarded as, in a manner, sacred to the souls in purga-

up from one end to the other by wax tapers, on which occasions the friars assembled there after supper to sing litanies for the repose of the souls of their predecessors whose remains are deposited in this convent cemetery. The strange appearance which the catacombs themselves present, the darkness broken by the flickering light of the tapers, the mediæval aspect of the friars, and their deep bass chaunt, all combined to form an unusual and striking spectacle. Happening one morning to visit these catacombs with a young friar in apparently robust health, he said to me as we came out, "We shall all be like this soon," pointing to the ghastly skeletons. Within a fortnight this same friar lay, as was thought, on his death-bed. After being in great peril, however, and undergoing several severe relapses, he finally recovered; and before leaving Rome, I had the satisfaction of ascending to the top of the dome of St. Peter's in company with him.

tory; Thursday to the Sacrament of the Eucharist; Friday to the Passion of Christ; and Saturday to the Virgin Mary.

THE CLOTH FACTORY.

The convent I am describing, being the chief Capuchin house of the Province of Rome, has attached to it as previously mentioned, an "Infermeria" or hospital for sick friars, and also a pharmacy, together with one or two monastic apothecaries. The sick are not placed in wards, but each patient has a separate cell, the conventual system being thus retained even in the hospital. The infirmary contains a couple of chapels where mass is celebrated daily for the benefit of the patients. Most of these, however, were aged and infirm persons who, being invalided, were allowed to pass the remainder of their days in the enjoyment of the greater comforts, especially in the matter of diet, which the hospital affords.

An interesting part of this extensive convent is the cloth factory, where the cloth required for the habits of all Capuchins in the Province of Rome is manufactured. I have often watched the successive stages of this process with attention and profit. Some of the friars labour here, and under their direction several secular workmen and boys are likewise employed. The habits, that is the cassock and cloak worn by the Order, are served out to the community once in three years, but each person has to do the requisite sewing for himself, the cloth when delivered to the friars from the factory being cut out but not made up. Another small factory is devoted to cutting into proper shape the leather used for making the sandals that form the only covering for their feet.

Attached to the convent is a considerable space of garden-land, which is chiefly cultivated for vegetables, of which such an abundance is raised that besides an ample daily supply for the numerous community throughout the year, a large quantity is sent for sale to the Piazza Navona, the well-known fruit market of Rome. About a score of common labourers were employed in tilling the soil under the directions of a lay-brother. The cultivation of this land was a specimen of good gardening; every yard of ground being used, and not a weed to be seen. I have already alluded to the flower gardens in the centre of the two cloisters. There is likewise a botanical garden in which medicinal plants for the pharmacy are produced. Apropos of gardens, I may mention that a little plot of ground was allotted to each of the Quæstors ("Questionarii" in Latin, or lay-brothers appointed to beg alms for the support of the brotherhood) which they themselves cultivate, and of the produce of which they occasionally give a little to the benefactors of the convent as a small return for their charity. If, however, the friars subsist upon the free offerings of the people—and their Rule does not permit them to have revenues—they are, in their turn, most charitable to the poor, even out of the scanty means at their disposal. It is the habitual practice in Capuchin convents to serve out soup to the poor at the monastery gate at noon daily. Very many times, and in different convents, have I seen this done. Indeed, the great iron cauldron of steaming soup standing at the cloister gate, with a friar ladling out its contents to an eager crowd of poor people, is among the most pleasing associations I retain in connexion with convent life; and one, too, which as much as anything else suggests to the memory the monastic system of the middle ages, of which charity towards the poor is allowed to have been a conspicuous feature, even by those most opposed to that system on principle.

Whilst I was at the Convent of La Concezione two of the friars there were painters, the studio of one of whom I have often visited, and seen the artist at work in his conventual habit, recalling the days when the church was the chief patron of the arts, and monks the foremost in the practice of them. One of these monastic artists, Padre B—, was a young German, and a highly intelligent man.

Here I end this very imperfect account of my visit to the Capuchin Convent at Rome. So entirely absent from my thoughts was any purpose of publishing my impressions of this visit that I took no notes at the time, or I should be enabled to enter into many details which the want of memoranda prevents my now doing. I can scarcely hope to have succeeded in conveying to the reader's mind a full idea of the picturesqueness of this monastery and everything connected with it, or of the quiet even tenour of life led there. I shall ever look back with pleasure on the period passed within its walls. It would be difficult to forget (*inter alia*) the unusual and impressive associations connected with the midnight Office, and with the long and dimly-lighted corridors along which one had to thread one's way in order to reach the church at that solemn hour; or the many pleasant strolls the author has had in the " cool monastic shade" of the cloisters, or in the well-tilled convent gardens. And more difficult still would it be to forget the cheerful, hospitable men whose guest, for several months, he had the good fortune to be.

CHAPTER VI.

State of Clerical Education and Monastic Discipline in Italy.

It has been mentioned in the preceding chapter that at the period of my visit to the Convent of La Concezione, it contained a "study" or class of sacred eloquence, as it is called, comprising thirteen students all of them in holy orders. By "Sacra Eloquenza" or sacred eloquence is meant the Art of Preaching, which is made a subject of special study by those of the Italian clergy who intend to practise that branch of the clerical profession. Preaching forms an important duty with many of the religious Orders, and particularly so in the case of the Capuchins. During Lent and Advent, Capuchin convents are often deprived of as many as a third of their numbers, who proceed by appointment with the parish-priests, to particular parishes, to deliver a course of sermons either daily, or twice or thrice a week. The humble, poor appearance of these friars— for they preach in their ordinary monastic habit—combined with their well-known severity of life and religious zeal, usually attracts large audiences. It is hardly necessary to observe that the priests, or Padri, alone are allowed to preach, and only such of these as have studied with a view to appearing in the pulpit, and have thus earned for themselves the title of "Predicatore" or preacher. The practice of weekly preaching does not so generally prevail as in England, but this is partly compensated for by a series of long and carefully prepared sermons at particular seasons, especially in Lent and Advent. I have been given to understand by some of these preachers, that they write their sermons at length, and then commit them to memory, and that they do this even when they have to deliver a course of daily sermons. These discourses, of which I have heard many at Rome, Naples, Genoa, and other places, usually occupy a full hour in the delivery.

While touching upon the study of eloquence

as a preparation for the pulpit, I will take the opportunity of adding a few words on the general studies pursued among the religious Orders. The lay-brothers are not expected to be literate or "dotti," as they themselves say, but from the Padri a long course of preparatory study is required. When the twelve months' novitiate is concluded, the course of study for the priesthood commences, and usually continues for six or seven years. It is necessary for candidates for holy orders to be fair Latin scholars at the outset, the text books they have to read being mostly in that language. The first part of the course is that of philosophy, under which head are included subjects not specially connected with any profession, but intended to impart general culture to the mind. The term "philosophy" in this technical sense, as a course of general education, is more common in continental schools and universities than in English. The principal subjects comprised under this head appear to be logic, natural theology, mathematics and physics. The philosophical course usually occupies two years, and of the remaining period of about four years, the first half is devoted to dogmatic theology, and the second to moral philosophy, especially in its application to the duties of the confessional.

The duties that devolve on the clergy as confessors, are studied with great minuteness, and are apparently reduced in respect of system and precision to something of the form of an ethical science. Numerous treatises have been written on this subject, in which every part of a confessor's duties are explained in much detail. Friars studying for holy orders are frequently sent from convent to convent, according as they require to pass from one subject to another, particular monasteries often having "studies" or classes for some one branch of learning only. This convent may have a study or class of philosophy, a second of dogmatic theology, a third of moral philosophy, and a fourth, as in the case of the Convent of La Concezione, of elocution.

Such is the course of study usually pursued in the monastic Orders by candidates for the priesthood. Before quitting this subject, I will venture to make one or two remarks upon the state of education prevalent among the Italian clergy generally so far as my means of observation enable me to form an opinion, although I do so with diffidence, being convinced that a traveller visiting a foreign country for a few months, or a year, cannot be competent to pronounce a confident opinion on a question of this nature, even though he may have enjoyed greater opportunities of forming a judgment than fall to the lot of most travellers.

I have known and conversed with members of the Roman Catholic clergy* of every degree, from the highest to the lowest—from Pope

---

* Among the Italian clergy whose acquaintance I made, was Padre Passaglia, author of the now famous *brochure*, on the temporal power of the Papacy. He was then a Jesuit, and Professor of Theology at the Roman College, whither all the Divinity students in Rome, of every nation, flocked to hear his Lectures, which were delivered in Latin. Padre Passaglia enjoyed the reputation of being one of the first theologians of the day. In Patristic Theology, especially, he is probably unsurpassed in Europe.

Pius IX. to the humble mendicant friar, including cardinals, archbishops and bishops, generals of monastic Orders, abbots, priors and other superiors of religious houses, parish priests and curates, and monks and friars of a large number of Orders. Speaking then from my personal knowledge and observation of the Italian clergy, I am of opinion that they are usually well versed in the several subjects of their professional studies. They are good Latin scholars, and well read in dogmatic theology. Their Latin scholarship, however, is for the most part based on modern and mediæval Latin, for the classical authors of antiquity, Roman as well as Greek, appear to be but little, if at all, studied by the Italian clergy generally. They also, as a body, unquestionably possess a full share of that sort of experience of men and things which is implied in the expression, a knowledge of the world. But there appears to be with the mass of the clergy, a want of that general reading on subjects unconnected with their professional studies which is essential to a high degree of mental culture. In this respect, however, the Italian clergy are not peculiar, for the same may be predicated of the bulk of the clergy of most, if not all, Christian sects. At the same time it is only just to add that among the Italian priesthood are to be found many men of deep and extensive erudition in addition to mere professional learning, in which latter as above mentioned, the great body of the clergy are not deficient. I make this criticism on the state of clerical education with more confidence than I should otherwise do, having noticed a confirmation of my opinion by one who, on such a subject, must be allowed to be an excellent authority, namely, a Vicar-General of the diocese of Paris, who published in 1856, a pamphlet in which he contends that the education of the Roman Catholic clergy is of too exclusively professional a character, and that this should give place in part to studies of a wider range.*

* I refer to this pamphlet from memory only, not having it at hand. Monseigneur Dupanloup, Bishop of Orleans, has also some excellent remarks in his work, 'De l'Education,' on the danger of sacrificing

It will perhaps be expected that I should give some opinion with regard to the present state of discipline among the religious Orders of Italy. On this point I may observe that if I have felt diffident in pronouncing an opinion, founded on my own experience, in respect of the state of education among the priesthood, much more must I hesitate in recording opinions upon a matter which is necessarily to a great extent removed from the opportunities of personal observation open to any traveller; especially as in this volume I endeavour to confine my remarks to what I have myself seen, or ascertained, to the exclusion, as far as possible, of merely hearsay testimony. Of course, however, I cannot avoid having formed some opinion on the subject; for, after spending many months in monasteries, and conversing with a great number and variety of clergy of all ranks and orders, as well as with numerous lay Roman Catholics, I could not fail to carry away some impression with regard to the state of morality,

general education to that of a special or professional character.

and the observance of monastic discipline generally, among the religious Orders.

That impression, whatever it may be worth, is that discipline and regularity of life are for the most part strictly observed in the convents of Italy, although doubtless there are many instances where individual members of a religious community lead a life little in accordance with the spirit of the monastic institution. I might add some remarks from instances that have fallen under my own observation, on the acknowledged difficulty felt by Superiors of convents in dealing with such cases when they occur, but this would lead me into too wide a digression.

As my opinion is founded in part on the conversation of monks and friars themselves, it may be as well to observe that I did not find it to be true, as many Protestants suppose, that the Roman Catholic clergy are always anxious to keep in the background, and even to deny, whatever facts might seem to militate against their order, or the monastic state in particular. So far is this from being the case, at least to the extent commonly supposed, that I have been

MONASTIC DISCIPLINE. 139

told by several members of the priesthood that among the numerous body of persons of which the Italian clergy consist (and it must be remembered that in a Catholic country like Italy, the clergy of all ranks and orders greatly exceed in number the clergy of any Protestant country) there are many who are total strangers to the spirit and practice of their religion.

In more than one instance, when I have expressed to a monk the satisfaction I felt in seeing such strict discipline and such apparent devotional feeling prevailing in monasteries, I have been met with the assurance that nevertheless cases often occur where persons dedicated to a religious life, retain little or none of the spirit of their vocation. "Vi sono dei buoni e dei mali," a friar once said to me, "quando un religioso osserva i regoli e le constituzioni dell' suo ordine, si sente una felicità veramente di paradiso che non può esprimersi; ma altrimente lo stato religioso non è un paradiso ma più tosto il contrario."*

* "Some are good and others bad. When a Religious observes the rules and constitutions of his Order, he feels truly a heavenly happiness that cannot be ex-

This friar was held in much respect by his Order, and was formerly the Superior of a convent; but his time of office having expired, he had since become a simple friar again.

From another member of a religious Order I heard that in one of the large cities of Italy, there were several priests leading notoriously irregular lives, after being suspended by the archbishop for their breaches of discipline. I could mention, were it worth while, other instances that came to my knowledge tending to show that there is not, among the clergy of the Roman Church, that determination to conceal and ignore everything adverse to themselves or their church, which is generally ascribed to them by their theological opponents. So far as regards the religious communities, at least, it would seem that they do not care to ignore the existence of occasional irregularities, being apparently conscious that such are the exceptions among a large body of men of generally exemplary lives.

pressed; but, otherwise, the religious state, so far from being a paradise, is rather the reverse."

CHAPTER VII.

Convents of Rome continued.

The number of religious houses of both sexes in Rome is very great. In most streets there is at least one convent, and many streets contain several. With a few exceptions, every Order has its principal house at Rome, which is the residence of its General and his staff of assistants for the government of the Order throughout the world. Each religious Order has some peculiar duties or observances distinguishing it from others; but, nevertheless, the general routine of life is very similar in most of them, while the conventual buildings are for the most part upon nearly the same plan, comprising the cloister, round which, on the first floor, are the dormitories and cells, with windows opening into the cloister—the refectory, the library, the garden, and the church. Having already given an account in some detail of one or two of these monastic establishments, it will be unnecessary to describe minutely each of the convents which I went over. We will, however, take a passing glance at the principal of those that I visited, which may assist in rendering more complete the reader's impressions of the conventual institutions of Rome generally.

One of the most interesting of these is the Carthusian Priory of Santa Maria degli Angeli, built on the site of Diocletian's Baths, part of the ruins of which has been incorporated into the monastery itself. Its church formed the great hall of the ancient thermæ, or baths. This monastery is remarkable for two beautiful cloisters, one of which is celebrated, and therefore often visited, while the other is little known to travellers, although well worthy of notice. The great cloister is the largest I have seen in or out of Italy, being on a scale out of all proportion to cloisters in general. Its colonnades are supported on *one hundred* marble columns. The effect of this magnificent cloister is very fine, on account of its vast size, which, combined with the simplicity of its construction, is characteristic of Michael Angelo, to whom we are indebted for this noble specimen of claustral architecture, as well as for the formation of the stately priory church from the remains of Diocletian's Hall. Michael Angelo is said to have commemorated the erection of this cloister by planting four cypresses in the middle of the immense open space which it encloses. Of these trees, three are still standing, but the fourth having been blown down, has been replaced by a young cypress grown from the seed of one of the old trees. The second cloister also is most beautiful, although quite different in character from the other. It is comparatively small, but exceedingly elegant in its style of architecture, which is exhibited to great advantage by the care and taste with which the garden in the centre is laid out. The first cloister is grand and imposing, the second graceful and beautiful.

The monks of this Certosa wear the usual white habit of the Carthusian Order. As in the case of some other Orders, the rather singular custom prevails of the lay-brothers allowing their beards to grow, although the Padri or priests are shaven. They rise to matins in the middle of the night, and, in accordance with the Carthusian practice, they chaunt the Canonical Hours of prayer very slowly and with marked emphasis. The Superior is styled Prior, monasteries of this Order having the rank and style of priories. In walking through the dormitories I was struck by their extreme narrowness, some of them being barely wide enough to admit of a person passing through them, which, I presume, is attributable to their having been constructed, or adapted to monastic purposes, from ancient ruins. In one of the corridors I noticed a board suspended from the wall with an announcement on it to the effect that on that day or the next would be held "la baccata," an expression signifying, I believe, a "general washing of linen." I took note of this, because insignificant as the circumstance was, it served nevertheless to illustrate the systematic regularity of a conventual *ménage*, and because it called to mind the domestic life of a religious community as distinguished from the artistic and mediæval associations connected with monastic institutions. The Carthusians, called in Italian " Certosini," will be more particularly noticed when we describe the famous priory of the Order near Pavia.

Not far from the Certosa of Santa Maria degli Angeli is the Cistercian Abbey of San Bernardo, situated in the Piazza dei Termini. Its church is very ancient, and is in form a rotunda, bearing so far a resemblance to the Pantheon. Some antiquaries believe it to have formed a part of the neighbouring Baths of Diocletian, although others suppose it to have been a temple. The Cistercians, like the Benedictines, (of which order indeed they are a reformation), the Carthusians, the Regular Canons of St. Austin and others, are monks strictly so called, as distinguished from the friars on the one hand, and the congregations of Regular Clerks on the other; for the numerous religious Orders of men may be conveniently classified under one of the three leading divisions of monks proper, who were mostly instituted before the thirteenth century; the friars, with their several reformations, founded chiefly from the thirteenth to the sixteenth century; and the Regular Clerks (such as the Theatins, Jesuits, Barnabites, Crociferi, Scolopi, &c.), the earliest Order of whom, the Theatins, was instituted soon after the commencement of the Reformation, when zealous efforts were made to instil renewed life and usefulness into the monastic system. The Cistercians wear a white habit and black scapulary, except the lay-brothers, who have a brown habit, very similar to that of the Franciscans. Their monasteries have mostly the rank of abbeys, and are usually presided over by mitred abbots. The Cistercian rule, as instituted by St. Bernard, was an exceedingly strict one; but some of its more rigid ordinances have become a good deal mitigated, except in the case of the Reformed Cistercians, commonly called Trappists,* who

* The congregation of Reformed Cistercians, or Trappists, now comprises about thirty houses, the most numerously tenanted of which is the Abbey of

follow St. Bernard's rule in its original severity. In the Abbey of San Bernardo, I saw an interesting gallery of engravings, consisting chiefly of heads of philosophers and other eminent men of antiquity. The Cistercians possess a particular interest for English travellers, from the fact that a large proportion of the monasteries in England at the Reformation were of that Order. The Abbey of Santa Croce in Gerusalemme, adjoining the Basilica of the same name, is also Cistercian, and the head house I believe of the Order.

The Abbey of San Gregorio sul Monte Celio, beyond the Arch of Constantine, is finely situated on the Cœlian Hill, whence its name

Aiguebelle, near Montélimart, in the south of France, containing about two hundred and twelve monks. The Abbot of this stately Abbey is both mitred and crosiered. A new branch of the Cistercian Order has lately been founded in France, under the name of the Cistercians of the Immaculate Conception, the mother house of which is the Abbey of Sénanques, near Gordes, in the department of Vaucluse. Great activity seems to prevail at the present time in France in building and enlarging religious houses of nearly every Order.

is derived. It was from this monastery—or rather from one that stood on its site—that Pope Gregory the Great sent St. Augustine and other missionaries to convert the English to Christianity, a record of which event may be seen in a modern inscription on one of the columns of the church. This is approached through a four-sided court or cloister, constituting a sort of large vestibule to the church—a form of construction which may occasionally be seen in other Italian churches as in Sant' Ambrogio at Milan, and the Annunziata at Florence. In an adjoining garden are three chapels adorned with fine frescoes by Guido and Domenichino, and a statue of St. Gregory (the founder of these chapels and of the adjacent monastery), which was begun by Michael Angelo and finished by Nicolo Cordieri.

The Abbey of San Gregorio, although a spacious building, and with a better exterior than most Italian convents possess, contained only eleven monks at the time of my visit, of whom eight were priests, and three lay-brethren. I was shewn over the convent by one of the latter, a fair, vigorous-looking young man, who said that these were Camaldoli monks, a distinct Order from the Camaldoli Hermits. Respecting the former, I am not able to give much information, but some account of the hermits of this name will be given in a subsequent chapter. My informant told me that whereas the Camaldoli Hermits live alone in separate small houses within a common enclosure, these monks live in community, thus resembling most other religious Orders. They have a white habit, and a three cornered clerical hat of the same colour. San Gregorio is presided over by a mitred abbot. The late Pope, Gregory XVI., was a monk of this abbey, and an inscription on a stone tablet over one of the cells records that it was occupied by him.

A little higher up the hill than San Gregorio is the Convent of the Passionists, an austere Order, founded about the beginning of the present century by the Blessed Paolo-Maria. Although so recently instituted, it is very numerous, possessing many houses in Italy and other countries. The Passionists wear a black habit with a white cross upon it, and use only sandals for the feet. They rise to matins at midnight, and are noted for the slow and emphatic manner in which they recite the liturgy. They are reckoned among the most ascetic of the religious Orders. This convent is the head house of the Order, and as such the residence of the General, to whom I had an introduction. The convent garden is pretty, and has a charming view over the Coliseum and the Palace of the Cæsars. The religious community consisted of about seventy persons.

On another of the Seven Hills, the Aventine, stand the Church and Convent of Santa Sabina. The church is a stately edifice, erected on the foundations of an ancient temple, and adorned by twenty-four antique columns of Parian marble, besides four of granite in the portico, and a painting of some celebrity by Sassoferato. The convent contains spacious cloisters and a garden, from the latter of which one of the finest views over Rome may be obtained, with the Tiber flowing at the foot of the Aventine Hill, on the extreme edge of which you are standing. This convent is of the Dominican Order, and is famous for having been tenanted by St. Dominic himself, whose cell, now converted into a chapel, is shewn to visitors. The cell occupied by St. Pius V., when a Dominican friar, is also shewn, and like the former is now a chapel. In ascending the Aventine, on the left, before arriving at Santa Sabina, is a garden with its walks bordered by very tall and well trimmed evergreens. In this garden is a small but pretty church with a large mansion adjoining—the church, house and ground all belonging to Cardinal F——, in his capacity of Grand Prior of the Knights of Malta,[*] who also enjoys revenues appertaining to the office. I was indebted to the Cardinal for advising me to see this interesting remnant of that celebrated Order, as well as the Convent of Santa Sabina. The little church of the Grand Priory was nearly destroyed during the siege of Rome by the French in 1849, but it had already risen again from its ruins a new

[*] The Grand Priory of the Knights of Malta was excepted from the general suppression of that Order.

and elegant building with a façade tastefully adorned with arabesques. The view of Rome from this garden is the same as that from Santa Sabina, with the advantage that this, being uncloistered, may be visited by ladies also.

The Barnabite Convent of San Carlo ai Catenari, in the old Jewish quarter of Rome, and the great Observant Convent of Ara Cœli on the summit of the Capitol, were likewise among those that I visited. San Carlo is a spacious and handsome convent, and is the "capo convento," or head house of the Barnabite Order. At the time of my visit, a general chapter of the whole Order was being held there, and among the "heads of houses" present was the Provost of San Bartolommeo degli Armeni, at Genoa, whom I was glad to have the opportunity of meeting again on this occasion. The stately church of this convent is a fine structure, and its magnificent dome is one of the largest in Rome, ranking in point of size, according to some, next after that of St. Peter's. The Observant Convent of Santa Maria in Ara Cœli is splendidly situated on the Capitol. It has a fine church approached by a flight of no less than one hundred marble steps of great width. The windows of the convent, owing to its elevated position, command an extensive view of Rome. The number of friars was then, as I was given to understand, about two hundred. It is the head house of the Order of Franciscan Observants, which is one of the most numerous in the world.

The Benedictine monastery of San Paolo fuori delle Mura, and the Capuchin Convent of San Lorenzo, have been already noticed in describing the Basilicas of San Paolo, and of San Lorenzo. The Jesuits have a large house at Rome, adjoining the well-known church of the Gesù; the Dominicans have the head house of their Order at Santa Maria sopra Minerva; the Theatins possess a convent adjoining the great church of Sant' Andrea della Valle, believed by some to stand on the site of Pompey's Curia, the scene of Cæsar's assassination; the Oratorians at the Chiesa Nuova, founded by St. Philip Neri; the bare-footed Carmelites at Santa Maria della Vittoria in the Piazza dei Termini;

and the unreformed Carmelites at Santa Maria Transteverina, between St. Peter's and the Castle of Sant' Angelo; the Augustinians have a convent in the Corso, and one of the two branches of that Order is, I believe, located at S. Agostino in the Piazza del Popolo; the Trinitarians, instituted by St John of Matha, at the church of La Trinità in the Via Condotti; besides whom, the Recollects, Minims, Crociferi, Scolopi, Lazarists, and very many others, together with a prodigious number of Orders of women, have one or more houses at Rome.

Of the numerous nunneries at Rome, I do not here speak for want of personal knowledge on the subject. I had, however, the advantage of entering two houses of uncloistered nuns, by the introduction, in each case, of friends of the sisterhood. One of these was a handsome convent in Transtevere, on the exterior of which were inscribed the words, "Monastero dei Sacri Cuori di Gesù e Maria." It has an elegant Gothic chapel, which is a great rarity at Rome. The other was the extensive monastery of La Trinità dei Monti, well known to travellers who have been at Rome, from its commanding position overlooking the Piazza di Spagna. It belongs to French nuns of the Order of the 'Sacré Cœur.' My friend (who was well known at the convent) and myself were admitted by a sister whose demeanour recalled Wordsworth's line:

"A nun demure, of lowly port."

The inmates of this monastery—that is, I presume, the choir sisters—are professedly all of noble birth.* It has a fine cloister, oblong in form; and the convent church is adorned by several celebrated paintings. These nuns have also a country house, or 'villa,' in the outskirts of Rome, on the road leading to the Villa Pamfili.

* The inmates of nunneries are divided into two bodies, the Choir Sisters and Lay Sisters, corresponding respectively to the Padri and Lay Brothers in convents of men.

CHAPTER VIII.

Pedestrian Excursion to rural Convents.

On the morning following the feast of the Ascension—on which day I had seen the Pope assist in state at High Mass in St. John Lateran, and afterwards give his benediction from the Loggia, over the west entrance, to the crowd assembled in the Piazza beneath—I set out upon a short pedestrian tour to the country district lying contiguous to Rome, on the south or Neapolitan side. I intended to walk first to Frascati, where I had an introduction to the Superior of a monastery. I left Rome by the Porta San Giovanni. The Campagna in the neighbourhood of this gate is intersected at various points by remains, in different states of preservation, of the Roman aqueducts, which are among the most beautiful of the monuments of classical antiquity. The appearance of the Campagna is that of an immense undulating plain covered generally with verdure, parts of it here and there being cultivated, but almost entirely without human habitations. At a distance of about twelve miles from the Porta San Giovanni, rise the Alban Hills, on the acclivity of one of which stands Frascati; and beyond, on another of the hills, is Albano, deriving its name from the ancient Alba, familiar to students of Roman history, although the site of the Latin city, Alba Longa, is believed to have been higher up, on the lake itself, where Palazzola now stands. The vestiges of classical times still to be seen at Albano, seem, however, to imply the existence here of an ancient town. The present town was built in the 15th century. The middle-age walls and gateways still remain, and placed as they are at the top of the long ascent by which Albano is approached from Rome, give to the place quite a picturesque effect. Indeed, you feel unwilling to allow yourself to be persuaded that they are not a portion of the walls of Roman days, so time-worn do they appear. I missed taking the road that leads to Frascati, and did not find out my mistake until I was near Albano, having been set right by two mounted dragoons, whom I met patrolling the road. I then determined to proceed thither at once, leaving Frascati to be seen on the return journey. This, as the event proved, was rather a fortunate mischance than otherwise.

The Lake of Albano, anciently Alba, is situated at a considerable elevation; for high as is the position of Albano itself, more lofty still is the lake, which you reach by a steep ascent from the town. Arriving, when at the summit of this ascent, upon the edge of the lake, a most lovely view lies before you. At the top of the hill or mountain is an immense basin, supposed to have been the crater of an extinct volcano, forming the Lake of Albano, whose deep blue water vies in richness of colour with the Italian sky above; and around the sides of the lake rise, in varied forms of beauty, steep and thickly wooded banks, with here and there a mule-path winding its way among them. On one side of the lake, to the left, is perched the small town of Castel Gandolfo. Within the little town stands conspicuously a country palace belonging to the Pope, thoroughly mediæval in character. The charming view presented to the traveller, standing on the side of the lake immediately above Albano, is heightened by the pretty convent of San Francesco, whose walls are almost washed by the waters of the lake. The view thus slightly sketched, with an Italian sun and sky to illustrate the whole, was delightful beyond description.

To the Superior of this convent, I had a letter of introduction. Glad indeed was I to arrive at its hospitable gate, after a walk of sixteen miles, having breakfasted only on a cup of *caffé nero*, and a piece of dry bread. I was told that the Superior was away, having gone to the neighbouring city of Velletri to take part in a festival to be held there on the morrow. I stood a few moments in the charming little cloister of the convent, awaiting the Vicar, or vice-principal, who had been sent for from his cell. On his arrival, I presented my letter of introduction, and inquired whether I might lodge a night in the convent. "E perchè no?" ("and why not?") was his reply. "But," he added, "this with us is a fast day, and we shall therefore, I fear, have little to offer you." This difficulty, however, was easily got over, on my remarking that, when sojourning in a monastery, I expected, as a matter of course, to conform to its rules.

Never shall I forget the agreeable impressions of that afternoon. Extreme natural beauty seemed to combine with historical associations to add interest and pleasure to the scene. If the scenery in itself was lovely, the effect was increased by vivid associations with a bygone epoch. There was the same romantic interest as that excited by a saunter through any of the ruined abbeys of England, but without that feeling of melancholy which is naturally raised by the sight of the demolition of what once formed habitations of men and women, and the scene of the mingled joys and miseries of human life, whether the ruin be a classical or a mediæval one. Here, amid enchanting scenery, I beheld—not a ruined cloister, a ruined refectory, or a dilapidated church; but cloister, refectory, dormitories, cells, and church all in perfect preservation, and devoted to the purposes for which they were originally built; and tenanted, too, by a brotherhood, whose personal appearance and mental character seemed equally mediæval with the buildings they inhabited.

Having partaken of a frugal meal in the refectory, and reposed for a time on a tiny monastic bed in a proportionately tiny cell overlooking the lake, I rose, and throwing open the linen window, leant on its sill, thoroughly taking in and enjoying the view and the associations of the place. In the flower garden, under my window, sat a black-clad secular priest conversing with a friar who stood near him caressing a diminutive tortoiseshell kitten, over whose little life one moon could scarcely have passed. After a while I joined them. Observing several other specimens of infant Grimalkins in the garden, I inquired of the friar what was the object of having so many, to which he replied "Per dare ai benefattori," (to give to our benefactors), from which I infer that even a convent puss is esteemed more highly than another by the "fedeli." As we were speaking, that pleasant sound, the convent bell, began to vibrate on the ear, calling the community to evening Office; when the priest taking his leave, I accompanied the friar into choir to hear the service. It consisted of the last of the seven Canonical Hours, called Complin, followed by the "Litany of the Virgin," and reading aloud from a devotional book, concluding with silent meditation.

Two or three of the brotherhood afterwards conducted me into the pretty wooded "villa" or convent garden, whence they showed me some charming views. They also pointed out to me a stone seat on which Pope Gregory XVI. had sat when he visited the convent from his neighbouring palace at Castel Gandolfo. I think they said that the late Pope had made as many as eight visits to this monastery. On my happening to inquire whether the whole of the large garden was within the "clausura" (that is, the point beyond which women are not admitted) one of the friars, after replying in the affirmative, added laughingly that he remembered two ladies having once visited the convent and its gardens, and having even been allowed to enter the dormitories and cells. These were a princess and a duchess, whose names he mentioned, but which I do not call to mind, and who came provided with a Papal Brief authorizing their admission.

The town of Albano itself is small, and depends for its interest upon that derived from its name, its position, and its picturesque walls. Numerous vestiges of classical times moreover may be seen in its neigbourhood. It is a bishop's see, which is always filled by a cardinal. The cathedral was undergoing extensive repairs at the time of my visit, so that I could not judge of its merits. Great activity seemed to prevail in the Papal States in repairing and decorating churches, and even new ones might occasionally be seen in course of erection, notwithstanding the vast number already existing. St. Bonaventura, the disciple of St. Francis, and surnamed the " Angelic doctor," was Bishop of Albano.

As several of the friars were to leave on the

following morning for Velletri, to take part in the festival about to be celebrated there in honour of the Madonna, I determined to accompany them. Instead of proceeding by the highroad, a distance of eleven miles, they led me by a shorter way over the Alban Hills along rough and narrow mule-paths, ascending and descending alternately through beautiful woods or over turf-covered plains. No sooner had we got fairly *en route*, than the friars, some four or five in number, began to recite aloud, as they continued their walk, some prayers consisting of the "Litany of the Virgin," a few psalms, and one or two collects, a practice general among them on commencing a journey, however short. A form of prayer said on such occasions is known by the name of " Itinerarium clericorum." As we crossed the Alban Hills, it chanced that one of my monastic companions, a young broad-faced Swiss, was conversing with me in Latin, so that in passing this classic region I not only had the associations of ancient days present to my mind, but my ears also were gratified by the sonorous sounds of the noble language which takes its name from this very tract of country—Latium, of which Alba was the capital. We debouched from the mountain paths on to the highway a little before reaching Velletri—the Velitræ of the Romans, and before its conquest by them an important city of the Volsci.

We were bound to a convent perched upon a hill overlooking the town, the ascent to which commences at a wooden cross on the left hand just before Velletri. On arriving at the convent gate, the friars, in whose company I was, knelt down, during the interval that elapsed before it was opened, and offered a thanksgiving for their prosperous journey. On entering the monastery, they proceeded to wash their feet, "alla lavanda," as they termed it—it being the practice to offer warm water for that purpose to any barefooted friar who arrives at a convent after a journey.

In 1849 this convent was made an important position by the King of Naples in his operations against Garibaldi and the Republicans, who nearly destroyed it by their cannonade.

The King withdrew his army during the night, leaving the friars in great consternation lest they should be ill-treated by the Republican leader, for which, however, the result proved there was no cause. These facts were communicated to me by a friar at Rome, who was an inmate of the convent at the time. His health was seriously shaken by the alarm caused by the events in question, and he has been subject to severe epileptic fits ever since.

I was struck by the new and perfect state of the pretty little cloister and of the monastic buildings generally, and on my inquiring how the ravages of the artillery had been so quickly effaced, I was informed that the restorations had been made entirely by public subscription. The friars appeared to feel a just pride in this evidence of their popularity, which even the political excitement that has prevailed of late years in Italy, and in the Roman States in particular, has not diminished. Finding that a large addition to the ordinary religious community had already been made, and was likely to be still farther increased by numerous arrivals from the surrounding convents of the Order, with a view to assist in the festival of that and the following day, I took up my quarters in the town at the Albergo della Posta; frequently visiting the convent however, and those of its inmates with whom I was, or became, acquainted.

Among these was a young friar who had studied English, and who had acquired considerable proficiency in the language, being able to speak it fairly, as well as read it. He proved, moreover, to be a first-rate Latin scholar, and some Latin correspondence with which he subsequently favoured me, may be called, without exaggeration, a model of composition. When I visited Rome in the following year, I found that this friar had been sent to the Capuchin Convent there, to study foreign languages in the College of the Propaganda, it being intended, I presume, to turn his linguistic talents to account for missionary purposes. Many an English traveller on seeing this Franciscan—who, like the rest of his Order, wore a habit of coarse brown serge and sandals on his feet—would not hesitate to speak of him half contemptuously, half pityingly, as a poor, ignorant, begging friar; and yet Padre I——, mendicant though he be, is a highly educated gentleman, and fit to associate on terms of intellectual equality with scholars of any nation.

Velletri is an episcopal town of moderate size. It contains a palace of some celebrity, usually visited by travellers, and several churches and convents. There are also one or two picturesque old Italian towers, which accord with the generally old fashioned aspect of the place. The gate on the Roman side is of recent construction, but the gateway and wall towards Naples appear to date from many centuries back.

On the first Sunday of May is celebrated at Velletri a great festival in honour of *La Madonna delle Grazie*, so called from the many graces and favours supposed to have been obtained by prayers to the Virgin for her intercession, when offered before an image of her preserved in the cathedral, which is of wide local celebrity. This image is arrayed in queenly robes, and adorned with jewels of great price. An ecclesiastic of rank pointed them out to me, at the same time mentioning the reputed value of each. A cardinal presented one set, he said, worth so many thousand *scudi;* a bishop gave another, and so on. The clergy and laity from the neighbouring towns and villages came in large numbers to take part in the festival; some of the former, indeed, having come from as far as Rome. It was a sight worth seeing. The vespers in the cathedral on the eve of the festival were performed with great solemnity, the church at the same time presenting a gorgeous spectacle to the eye, from the profusion of rich tapestry and hangings with which every part was hung, and the countless wax lights suspended in glass chandeliers from the roof to the pavement, tall ladders being called into requisition to admit of those at the top being lighted. A grand procession, which is the leading feature of this festival, was to have taken place that evening after vespers, but was deferred till next day on account of bad weather.

On the following morning, being Sunday, a Pontifical High Mass was celebrated in the cathedral. In the afternoon the procession, which was of prodigious length, proceeded from the cathedral, along the principal streets of the town, passing through masses of people whose religious zeal was enthusiastic to a degree I never before witnessed or heard of on such an occasion. The procession commenced with a long succession of schools and confraternities, each of the latter headed by its banner; after which came deputations from some of the religious Orders preceded by their respective crosses. These were followed by the secular or parochial clergy and the chapter of the cathedral. Then came the Bishop in pontifical vestments; and lastly the aforesaid image of the Madonna was carried on the shoulders of several men, while in the meantime bands of music played and the clergy chaunted alternately.

It would be difficult to describe the effect produced on the assembled multitude by the sight of this image, which, as observed above, is held in high veneration in all the country round. No sooner did it come within view than the enthusiastic crowd not only fell on their knees, but seemed to be literally agitated by the intensity of their feelings of devotion to the Mother of Christ, as represented to their minds by the image. Hands were extended in attitude of prayer; eyes were fixed with reverential gaze on the image; sounds of supplication became more or less distinctly heard in different parts of the assembled mass, until, as the image was borne past the spot where I was, a universal cry or shriek proceeded from the kneeling crowd around me; that is to say, a vehement ejaculation of a devotional kind burst forth from the multitude, accompanied by a leaning forward of the whole body and a pressure of the hands together as if in earnest supplication. I thought at one moment they would have lost all restraint and have rushed to embrace the feet of the Madonna. I never before witnessed such a scene of religious excitement; and, indeed, this festival at Velletri appears to be considered exceptional, even at

Rome, for on my return I was asked whether I had heard the "gridi"—the "cries"—during the procession on this occasion.

I left Velletri on foot intending to return to Rome, viâ Frascati. Soon after quitting the prim modern gate of this antiquated-looking town, I overtook three Capuchin friars, to whom I introduced myself, as known to some of their Order at the convent on the hill above, and we joined company. Scarcely had we done so than we were overtaken by two other friars, with whom I had become acquainted during the previous days. According to their usual practice on commencing a journey they recited aloud, as they proceeded, a litany, some psalms, and a few prayers, by way of invoking a blessing.

I did not long enjoy the advantage of my monastic friends' company, our roads lying different ways. I had an agreeable walk of eleven miles to Genzano, situated upon the high road to Rome; and after a long and tiring, but pleasing, ascent from the town by a road bordered with double rows of limes, pruned into a uniform shape, I found myself at the gate of a pretty little convent at the top of the hill, overlooking the beautiful Lake of Genzano, the same, I believe, as that also known by the name of the Lake of Nemi. I had been recommended to visit this monastery by a friar of the community here, whom I happened to meet at Velletri. This friar, a venerable-looking man with a grey beard, is a painter, and the church of his convent is adorned by several of his pictures. In the temporary absence of the Superior, the vicar, or vice-principal, shewed me the convent and its pretty gardens, the view from which over the lake is most charming. This lake, like that of Albano, is situated at a considerable elevation, and is three miles in circumference. I was invited to dine with the friars in the refectory, which I did, and having rested sufficiently to resume my journey, I proceeded on my way to Frascati, by Albano, passing *en route* through the village of Aricia, which bore the same name in classical times, and was Horace's first halting place on his journey to Brundisium.

" Egressum magna me excepit Aricia Roma,
 Hospitio modico . . . ."

At Aricia was a famous grove sacred to the nymph Egeria.

In addition to these sources of interest derived from antiquity, is a magnificent viaduct stretching across the beautiful wooded dell, where, possibly, may have been Egeria's grove. This bridge is built of stone, and is broad, high, and of great length, deserving to be classed among the finest works of the kind. It has been constructed by the present Pope, as a Latin inscription indicates. The expense of its erection, together with that of two other handsome although smaller viaducts, (both of them built by Pius IX), on the same road towards Albano, must have been very heavy; indeed, it seems surprising that in the overburdened state of the Papal exchequer, consequent upon the political events of the last few years, means should have been found to defray the cost not only of the useful public works in question, but of others in various parts of the Pontifical dominions.

My good friends at the convent at Albano, where I called in passing, pressed me much to stay the night with them, but being desirous of hastening on towards Rome, I was obliged to content myself with resting there an hour or two and hearing the friars sing vespers, although I would gladly have tarried longer. The Superior insisted on sending a lay-brother to put me in the right road for Frascati, which was my next destination.

That road—the earlier part of which especially, skirting the lake and delightfully shaded by ilexes, is very beautiful—lay through the small but middle-age town of Castel Gandolfo with old castellated walls and gateways. This little town has already been mentioned as within view of the convent at Albano, and as containing the Pope's country palace. As we were passing through the gate on leaving the place, a voice exclaimed, " Povero miserabile ! datemi un baiocco per amor di Dio." On turning round, I saw a grated window by the side of the gateway, and standing at it was a man from whose mouth these words had proceeded. Another man was lying upon a bed within the room. In answer to a question from me, the prisoner did not deny the justice of his incarceration, replying candidly enough, "Per aver battuto un uomo." I gave him some baiocchi, and continuing our route, my companion and I soon after parted company, he returning to his cloistered abode, whilst I pursued my way towards Frascati, passing at a short distance from Castel Gandolfo, through a pretty wood, and subsequently through the village of Grotta Ferrata.

Frascati, an episcopal town on the acclivity of the Alban Hills, about twelve miles from Rome, is well known to travellers from the many large villas in its neighbourhood, which are resorted to by the more opulent inhabitants of Rome during the hotter months of the year. Like many of the provincial towns of the Papal States, Frascati has a mediæval aspect imparted to it by its quaint gateways, but the general appearance of the place is more flourishing than that of most towns of its size in this part of Italy. I was bound to a convent situated on the side of a mountain behind Frascati, and at the close of a long day's walk, the additional fatigue of the steep ascent was considerable. While I was toiling through the upper and more hilly part of the town, I noticed in a bye-street an old man sitting outside the door of a shop busily engaged in mending shoes. He was singing, and as I stopped for a moment to listen, I caught the following words which he sang in a loud, clear voice from a well known Latin hymn:

> " Ave maris stella,
> Dei mater alma,
> Atque semper virgo,
> Felix cœli porta."

Pursuing my way up the hill, and passing one or two large palaces, I arrived at the convent, which stands at a high elevation on the thickly wooded side of one of the Alban Hills, immediately behind Frascati. I was introduced to the Guardian, whom I found in one of the corridors, or dormitories, engaged in some carpentering operation. After reading the letter of introduction I had brought, and saying a few words to one of the friars, he beckoned me to be seated, and quietly and in perfect silence resumed the manual labour on which he had before been employed. The friar to whom he had spoken soon returned, whereupon the Superior, bidding me follow him, led me to a cell that had, by his orders, been prepared for me. This cell contained the usual furniture, consisting of a bed, table and chairs, together with a crucifix and an immense Breviary, equal in size to a large Bible. We had scarcely entered the cell, when the convent bell commenced ringing for complin, the concluding Office of the day, and the Guardian forthwith took his leave.

After service, the brotherhood repaired to a small but pleasant refectory, whither I was invited to accompany them. Grace being said in the ordinary form, the friars seated themselves on the benches placed against the walls with long narrow tables in front of them, and partook of their frugal " cena," during which a succession of the junior members of the community read aloud in turn for the general edification. Supper ended, they repaired to a neighbouring apartment, (which was, I believe, the convent kitchen) containing a blazing wood fire which proved most acceptable, for although it was now the month of May, a bitterly cold wind had prevailed for some days. Here they sat for a time "in recreazione," conversing in a subdued tone. I was glad to adjourn early to my little conventual bed, and to sleep off the fatigue of the day's walk; yet I did not sleep so soundly, but that I was aroused by the matin bell, and the "troccolo" or rattle already described as being used on these occasions to wake up somnolent friars. Hastily throwing on my clothes, I proceeded along the dimly lighted dormitories to the choir, where I heard the friars recite their midnight Office.

On the next day, after dining in the refectory with the brotherhood at their usual hour of a quarter past eleven, I made the ascent of the mountain on the side of which the convent stands. At this considerable elevation are the remains of the ancient city of Tusculum. I had not got far from the convent on my way to Tusculum when I fell in with a friar carrying a stole, a vase of holy water and a book, and accompanied by an old woman. Recognising the worthy padre as one of the fraternity with whom I was staying, I inquired of him whither he was going. He replied that

the woman had fetched him from the convent
to pronounce a blessing over a field, preparatory
to sowing it with seed. I joined them, and on
arriving at the field in question, the friar put
the stole round his neck, and having asked the
woman how much of the land she wished to
have blessed, he opened the book, from which
he recited a few prayers, concluding the ceremony by sprinkling some holy water over part
of the field. The friar then returned to his
monastery, and I to my Tusculan route,
whence I had diverged in order to see this unpretending little religious ceremonial.

In ascending the mountain, I passed several
pieces of sculpture, placed by way of ornament
at the side of the path. Among these was a copy
of the Venus dei Medici at Florence. Near
Tusculum I met a Capuchin lay-brother descending the mountain, and leading a well-laden ass. "Ah!" I exclaimed in Italian,
"I know very well whither you are going, you
and your ass, you are bound for the monastery
below, and have your paniers full of cheese."
The good friar seemed mightily astonished
at my acquaintance with his affairs, until I told

him how I had heard at the convent of his having been sent out on the previous day with an ass, to beg cheese from the inhabitants of the surrounding country for the use of the community. We soon parted—to meet again at supper in the convent refectory. Not long afterwards I arrived at the ruins of Tusculum. A large number of scattered stones mark the site of this famous city, but the only building still standing is a small, though elegant amphitheatre in fair preservation. An inscription records that Pope Gregory XVI. ascended here during his pontificate in order to show these interesting ruins to the Queen of Sardinia, then on a visit at Rome.

On the afternoon of the day following I took leave of my kind hosts, not without an invitation from the Guardian to prolong my stay, or to return before finally quitting Rome. I left the friars in recreation in the garden after dinner, the Superior being engaged in reading aloud from a newspaper to several friars near him the particulars of the treaty then recently concluded between the belligerents in the Russian war. The convent, which was built of greyish stone and had an antiquated appearance, seemed to be flourishing, nor did apprehensions appear to exist of its being affected injuriously by political contingencies; for the pretty little monastery church was undergoing, internally, a complete course of restoration, involving of course considerable outlay. Unwillingly did I quit this quiet and peaceful abode, even though Rome was to be my destination. There I arrived the same evening after a fatiguing walk over the stone-paved road that stretches from the Alban Hills, across the desert-looking Campagna, to the Eternal City.

CHAPTER IX.

Festival of Corpus Christi—Audience of the Pope —Return to England.

THE festival of Corpus Christi fell this year towards the end of May, soon after my return from the pedestrian excursion described in the preceding chapter. I have heard it called the finest of the great ecclesiastical ceremonials at Rome, but although I cannot altogether concur in that opinion, it is undoubtedly a very grand and imposing spectacle. Corpus Christi day, as the name implies, is a festival in honour of the institution of the Sacrament of the Eucharist. The Roman Catholic Church sets apart one of the greatest festivals of the year in solemn commemoration of the doctrine of the real presence of Jesus Christ in that Sacrament; and it is of importance that those who wish to enter into the spirit of the religious ceremonial on the occasion in question should bear this fact in mind. However erroneous such a doctrine may appear to Protestants, it is a matter of fact that Roman

Catholics believe Christ to be personally present in the Eucharistic elements; therefore in exhibiting the Host in a stately procession to the veneration of the people, it is Christ to whom honour is intended to be paid, and for which purpose all the resources of religion and art are profusely lavished. If visitors to Rome were to enter more into the spirit of what they see, instead of attending only to the outward show, they would both understand and enjoy the religious ceremonies far more than they usually do. It is the union in the mind of the spectator, of devotional feeling (or at least a power to comprehend and appreciate that feeling) with the artistic beauty of these ecclesiastical ceremonies, that gives to them an impressive character, which mere sight-seers are in a great measure strangers to.

On the morning of Corpus Christi day (which falls on the Thursday after Trinity Sunday) all Rome was in that state of general movement from east to west—from the Corso and its neighbourhood to St. Peter's—which forms one of the associations connected with the great religious ceremonies at Rome. The

Via Fontanella Borghese, with its successive continuations under different appellations till you reach the Bridge of St. Angelo, was full of pedestrians and carriages of every sort hurrying towards the scene of action—the foot passengers often finding it not an easy matter to keep clear of the carriages in the narrow streets, innocent as these mostly are of any approach to side-pavements. Occasionally, too, the passage was rendered still more difficult by the ponderous red-painted coach of some cardinal, with three or four servants in smart liveries and cocked hats. On arriving at the Bridge of St. Angelo, unprivileged carriages were stopped by mounted dragoons, who lined the way from this point to the Piazza of St. Peter's. For nearly a week this Piazza had been in course of preparation for the grand procession of to-day. The procession commences at the Sistine Chapel in the interior of the Vatican Palace, and descending the principal staircase, called the Scala Regia, makes the circuit of the Piazza.

The Scala Regia (which is open to the public) is hung, during this festival only, with very beautiful tapestry, reputed to be among the finest work of the kind extant, and well worth attentive examination. The whole of the ground to be passed over by the procession, in making the circuit of the Piazza, was covered in by an awning supported on tall poles, around which evergreens were wreathed in a spiral form, the awnings themselves, too, being decorated with pieces of coloured materials. The houses in the square had either tapestry, or hangings of red and yellow cloth suspended from the windows. The procession began to move at about half-past eight. I was told that the Pope commences the celebration of Low Mass in the Sistine Chapel when the head of the procession starts, and that by the time he has concluded mass the rear is ready to move, in which he himself takes part. The Piazza was filled by a large crowd of spectators; and long rows of chairs were placed for hire, under cover of the awning, on either side of the course to be taken by the procession.

The procession commenced with a numerous train of school children, educated by various institutions, some dressed in white, others in black gowns. These children, as well as every other person in the procession, whatever might

FESTIVAL OF CORPUS CHRISTI. 187

be his rank or office, carried a lighted wax candle. Next came the religious Orders, each preceded by its own Cross, and in many instances by a banner also. There was a long and varied succession of these monks and friars, who indeed constitute one of the most characteristic and interesting portions of this procession. Among the religious fraternities present were the Capuchins,* with their brown serge habit, sandalled feet, and long beards; the Observants† and Recollects, also dressed in brown, but without beards; the Reformed Augustinians, or Austin Friars, (in Italian, "Agostiniani Scalzi," or barefooted), in a black habit and thick white cord round the waist; the Unreformed Augustinians, viz., the "Agostiniani Calzi," or shoe-wearing; the two branches of the Carmelites, that is to say, the Scalzi or Reformed Carmelites,‡ (called Teresiani, from their reformer, St. Teresa), and the Calzi,§ or

* From the Convents of La Concezione and S. Lorenzo fuori delle Mura.
† Convent of Ara Cœli on the Capitol.
‡ Convent of La Madonna della Vittoria, at the Fontana dei Termini.
§ Convent of Sta. Maria Transteverina near St. Peter's.

Unreformed Carmelites; the Dominicans,* in a mixed habit of white and black; the Conventuals,† or Unreformed Franciscans, robed in black, with a thin white cord round the waist; the Camaldoli monks,‡ (a distinct Order from the Hermits of the same name), habited entirely in white; the Benedictines,§ in black, and several others.‖ After the religious Orders followed the parochial clergy, in surplices and stoles, who, as well as the religious Orders, chaunted in a low solemn tone the hymn "Pange Lingua," usually sung on this occasion.

* Convents of Santa Maria sopra Minerva, Santa Sabina, and San Clemente.

† Convent of the 'Dodici Apostoli,' adjoining the Basilica of that name.

‡ Abbey of San Gregorio sul Monte Celio.

§ Abbey of S. Paolo fuori delle Mura, and San Callisto.

‖ Neither the Cistercians from Santa Croce in Gerusalemme, or San Bernardo, nor the Carthusians from Sta. Maria degli Angeli, were present. The numerous Orders of Regular Clerks (sometimes called 'Berrettanti' because they wear, when in-doors, the 'berretta,' or small square cap, like secular priests), such as the Theatins, Barnabites, Crociferi, Somaschi, Scolopi, &c., are exempted from attendance in processions.

Soon afterwards came the insignia of several of the Basilicas, resembling in form a large and lofty umbrella, carried by means of a tall pole through the centre, and made in some instances of cloth of gold, and in others of coloured materials, ornamented with gold lace, &c. Each of these insignia was preceded by a handsome Cross, and was followed by the choristers, chaplains, and canons of the Basilica to which it belonged. The chaunting of some of these capitular choirs was really beautiful, especially that of Santa Maria Maggiore, which appeared to be listened to by the crowd with marked attention and interest.

The great dignitaries of the church could now be seen issuing from the Vatican by the Scala Regia. First came the bishops, wearing their mitres and chasubles. These were followed by the cardinals, who, like the bishops, wore mitres and chasubles, as well as red cassocks, and shoes and stockings of the same colour, and rich lace surplices. At the side of every cardinal walked an attendant, carrying a circular red hat, with long strings suspended from it, similar to those in which cardinals are repre-

sented in pictures, although these are merely
emblematical of the cardinalitial dignity and
office; for the hats now worn by the cardinals
on state occasions, are in shape similar to the
three-cornered hats of ordinary priests, although
red in colour, and ornamented with gold lace.
Immediately after the Sacred College, the
successor of St. Peter himself approached,
raised aloft in the chair of state, the "Sedia
Gestatoria," and elevating the Host in a gold
remonstrance to the veneration of the assembled
multitude. On either side of the Pope were
carried the large and graceful fans, made of
ostrich feathers, familiar to all who have witnessed the ecclesiastical ceremonies at Rome.
Behind the papal *cortége* followed the Pope's
chamberlains, dressed in black velvet doublets,
and Elizabethan ruffled collars, with flat bonnets
on the head. These chamberlains, whose office
is honorary, are usually laymen of distinction.

The procession was closed by a brilliant staff
of military officers, and a numerous escort of
cavalry. During the progress of the procession
round the Piazza, the booming of artillery from
the neighbouring Castle of St. Angelo, the

pealing of bells, and strains of instrumental music, mingling with the chaunting of the numerous clergy, all combined to add life and interest to the spectacle; the brilliancy of the *coup-d'œil* being moreover heightened by the glittering effect of the rays of a scorching sun upon the motley mass of bright colours exhibited to the view. When the procession had entered St. Peter's, the Pope pronounced the Benediction from the high altar, holding the Sacrament in his hands, and making with it the sign of the cross over the people. His Holiness then left, and his example was followed by most English visitors, but in ignorance probably of the more than usually beautiful music that was to be performed in the choir after the interval of a few minutes, when a magnificent mass, musically speaking, was celebrated.

Less imposing indeed, but scarcely less interesting, are the processions of the Host through the streets of Rome, which take place morning and evening from different churches during the week, or octave, of Corpus Christi. On this occasion it is a pretty sight to see the processions winding through the narrow streets, the houses on each side decorated with red cloths and other hangings, while here and there a temporary altar is tastefully erected, *al fresco*, in the line of the procession. When the procession arrives before one of these chapels improvised for the occasion, the hymn "Tantum Ergo" is chaunted, after which the priest gives the benediction from the altar, with the Host in his hands, the people all kneeling the while. The celebration of this great festival of the Roman Church is brought to a close on the eighth or octave day, in the evening of which a grand Procession again makes the circuit of the Piazza of St. Peter's, the Sacrament being carried on this occasion by a cardinal, the Pope and the remainder of the cardinals following on foot. This procession is worth seeing, but it cannot of course be compared for pomp and ceremony with that on Corpus Christi day itself.

My sojourn at Rome was now drawing to a close. I was glad, before leaving, to accept the offer of Cardinal F— to introduce me to the Pope. Some delay occurred in obtaining an audience, for as nearly all strangers were quitting Rome, partly on account of Corpus Christi being over, and partly because of the hot weather setting in, there was an unusual number of persons desirous of being presented; and some of these were even leaving without an audience, rather than incur the necessary delay. However, I at last received a despatch from Monsignore Borromeo, the Grand Chamberlain, conveyed to the convent where I was staying by a dragoon, in which I was informed that "the Holiness of our Lord" would deign to give me audience at the Vatican on a given day, some instructions being printed in the margin, in regard to the costume in which visitors to the Pope's Court are expected to appear. It is customary for persons entitled to wear a uniform of any kind to appear in it; otherwise the Papal court dress approaches as nearly as possible to a clerical costume, consisting of a plain black suit and white neckcloth, and shoes—dress boots it seems not being admissible. Ladies also are dressed in black, and wear long lace veils.

At eleven o'clock on the day named, I proceeded to the Vatican, and on presenting my letter of invitation was conducted through a suite of apartments to the antichamber appointed for visitors on these occasions. First in order was a large and handsome hall, the "Sala dei Domestici," occupied by servants, in the Papal livery of red silk. The spacious ceiling was covered by paintings in fresco. Passing through this hall, I had to cross a succession of apartments with floors of coloured marble, highly polished, and painted ceilings. One of these was occupied by a batch of military officers, another by a knot of ecclesiastics, a third by officials of the Papal household, and so on. On arriving at an antichamber, I was requested to leave my hat and gloves, and then proceeded to the *salle d'attente*. Between this and the Pope's reception-room there was but one other apartment, which appeared reserved for great dignitaries, although they did not seem to be accommodated with chairs, like the οἱ πολλοί in the outer antichamber. Whilst I was waiting, several cardinals passed through, to or from an audience. They were dressed as on state occasions, in their scarlet robes, and as they passed by, every body present rose and bowed, and the "guardia nobile" on duty at the door presented arms.

In the inner antichamber was a prelate in a purple cassock and fine lace surplice, who introduced each visitor as his turn arrived. When mine came, the Monsignore threw open the door of the audience chamber, and, after kneeling, immediately closed the door, and left me alone with the acknowledged Head of some two hundred millions of Christians.

Pius IX. was dressed in a white cassock and cape, a white skull-cap, and red slippers. He was seated under a canopy, with a writing-table in front of him. The chamber was a small one, being used for private occasions such as to-day. It is usual for persons admitted to an audience to kneel at the door on entering, and again on approaching the Pope. Roman Catholics kiss the gilt cross on the red slipper, in token of acknowledgment of the spiritual character of him whom they believe to be the vicar of Jesus Christ, but Protestants are not required to do so, and may kiss his hand instead. The Pope made several inquiries respecting my country, how long I had been in

Italy, and *àpropos* of the recent festival of Corpus Christi, made some observations in regard to the great religious ceremonies of the church. When I mentioned "Corpus Christi," the Pope said "Si, Corpus *Domini*," by which name it is commonly known in Italy and in Spain, although, in the Roman Missal and Breviary, it is invariably printed "Corpus Christi." When the audience was over, his Holiness offered me his hand to kiss; and as I retired, he rang a bell near his chair, whereupon the door was immediately opened by the prelate in attendance, by whom I was conducted out.

A few days afterwards I left Rome for Florence and Pisa, whence I travelled by the fine Riviera road to Genoa. From Genoa I proceeded northwards across the Simplon pass, through Switzerland to England, where, after a six months' absence, I found myself once more amid the wooded hills and fertile plains of Kent, with the luxuriant hops bending beneath their heavily-laden fruit—a sight perhaps as beautiful to the eye, though not so poetical to the imagination, as the vineyards of Italy.

CHAPTER X.

Convent of San Barnaba.

HALF way up one of the semicircle of mountains, rising immediately behind Genoa, is situated the ancient Convent of San Barnaba, tenanted by Capuchin Friars. San Barnaba, like most houses of this poor and austere Order, has little to attract attention externally, although to the lover of the picturesque, points of interest are not wanting even in the exterior, especially when taken in connexion with the monastic and mediæval associations of the place. Such, for instance, is a pretty image of the Madonna placed conspicuously on the top of the high wall of the convent garden, and which is the first object connected with the convent that strikes the eye on approaching it from Genoa. Skirting this wall—over which is seen a grove of lofty cypresses, whose dark-tinted foliage and solemn aspect seem to accord with the religious character of the place—you reach a gateway leading into a small court, in which stands the convent church. By its side is a gate opening into the convent itself.

One morning in the beginning of February, 1857, I arrived at this monastery of San Barnaba, and after ringing the bell, and waiting during the rather long interval that usually elapses in the case of a convent between this process and an answer being made to it, there appeared an elderly friar,

"Bare-footed, in his frock and hood,"*

tall and spare, wearing the ordinary costume of his Order, viz., a habit or gown of coarse brown serge, reaching to the ankles, and a short cloak of the same material and colour. Over his head was drawn a hood or cowl. His feet were scantily protected by leathern sandles, which are always worn by the bare-footed friars, and from his waist was suspended on one side a rosary of small wooden beads, and on the other a thick cord with three knots in it at intervals, intended to typify the three chief monastic vows. Being already known to the Superior, I

* Lady of the Lake.

was at once conducted to his cell. He was a venerable-looking man, wearing a long bushy grey beard. I briefly reminded him of my having been introduced to him in the preceding year by a mutual friend, and of an invitation given to me by a friar of his convent to sojourn there in the event of my visiting Genoa again. "Ma, caro," he replied, "la cuaresima s'avvicina, e qui si mangia magro schietto, schietto."* To this and other objections of the same kind, I answered that I should be ready to conform to the conventual rules in all respects so long as I remained there, not excepting that on which he was most emphatic, viz., the necessity of being always within the convent walls by the Ave Maria, or sunset. Finally, he consented to receive me on a short visit.

In the course of the same day I found myself once more pleasantly located in a veritable monk's cell. The window had no glass, a piece of linen being made to serve instead. The furniture consisted of a table, (on which stood a large crucifix) a couple of chairs, a *prie-dieu*,

* "But, caro, Lent approaches, and here we fast most rigidly."

and a small bed. This cell, which was usually reserved for the Provincial when he made his periodical visitations, was the largest in the convent, and about double the dimensions of the ordinary cells, but in other respects similar to them. And now, merging my own personality in the monastic community whose guest I had the good fortune to be, I will endeavour to give an idea of the aspect presented by the interior of the convent itself, and of the manner of life pursued by its inmates. There is of course considerable similarity in the method of life prevailing in religious houses generally, and also in the appearance of the monasteries themselves, both externally and internally, but I think there is much in connexion with this small but ancient convent of San Barnaba with which the reader will be glad to be made acquainted, notwithstanding that some account of several other conventual establishments has been given in the preceding pages.

The convent gate at the side of the church, opens into a small cloister, and a short passage connects this with another and larger cloister behind. The walls of both cloisters are ornamented with paintings in fresco. One of these represents the Madonna in a sky-blue robe, receiving the homage of an old man dressed in a coat of the same celestial tint. At foot is the inscription, "Mater Misericordiæ." Another exhibits a Capuchin friar with a cadaverous-looking countenance, being comforted whilst at prayer by angels, one of whom, (who might pass for a young Cupid) is playing on a violin. A third has for its subject a Franciscan, who with a mingled expression of sweetness and reverence is caressing the child Jesus, on whom choirs of angels are attending. Opening into the second or inner cloister is a door leading to a staircase by which you ascend to the dormitories. Over this door, in a glass case, is a painted wooden image of Christ bound to the pillar, preparatory to being scourged. An image of the Madonna, with the inscription, "Causa nostræ lætitiæ," meets the eye in passing up the little staircase.

The dormitories as has been more than once explained, are long corridors about five or six feet wide, into which the cells of the friars open. These dormitories contain fresco paintings representing various religious subjects, and here and there a large crucifix placed against the wall. There are also curious and interesting statistical tables of the Order posted up, shewing the number of saints, of cardinals, bishops, &c., which it has produced. The cells are similar in point of dimensions as well as in their furniture and general appearance, to those of the Capuchin Convent at Rome. The dormitories extend round the quadrangle formed by the inner cloister, with cells on both sides, the cells on one side of the dormitories looking into the cloister, and those on the other over the open country. The refectory at San Barnaba consists of a long room, or hall, having the door at the lower end, and tables of polished oak extending along the two sides and the upper end. It contains many pictures, but they are all indifferent. The most remarkable are a curious old pannelled painting over the door, and a Last Supper. The latter, in addition to the usual small round loaves, represents a dish before the Saviour with a lamb upon it.

The convent church, although small, is rendered pretty by its rustic simplicity. This simplicity of character harmonizes well with the convent itself, in which are blended, with much effect, the lowly and simple with the beautiful and solemn. The Capuchin Order being forbidden altars of stone, as inconsistent with their profession of extreme poverty, use wood instead, and accordingly their churches often exhibit beautiful specimens of carved or inlaid wood altars. The high altar of San Barnaba, though not a fine specimen of the kind, is nevertheless worthy of notice, on account of the variety of woods used, and their high state of polish. The roof of the church also is made of wood. The pavement is formed almost entirely of tombstones with inscriptions on them. The church, small as it is, is full of paintings, but none of them call for particular mention. The choir, (which as usual in convents is behind the altar, and walled off from the church for the greater seclusion of the friars) likewise contains many pictures. Most of these are calculated to excite feelings of a mournful character, such as Christ being scourged; the Agony on Mount Olivet; and a Dead Christ. Between the choir and the little sacristy is a modern picture in bright colours of the Madonna, appearing to a numerous train of pious and meek-looking novices. In one of several small rooms or closets adjoining the church, (which there are in this and most convents for the monks to hear mass by means of loopholes in the wall, without seeing or being seen by the people in church) is an old picture of the Virgin, a copy of that of Loretto. An inscription on it records the following legend. Some two centuries ago, a young Capuchin who had lately made his religious profession, heard himself addressed as if by a voice emanating from this picture. He had intended, as the inscription proceeds to inform us, to receive the communion that morning, but such was his amazement and confusion that he feared to do so, until as he was praying apart, the Madonna spoke to him a second time, enjoining him to communicate with the others—" cogli altri." The inscription adds that after being for some time neglected and forgotten, this " miraculous " picture was placed in its present position in 1728.

The " villa," or convent garden, is both large and pretty. It would be more correct to say the gardens, which are connected by flights of stone steps leading from one to the other. One of these gardens contains numerous vines, as well as vegetables of various kinds; another, a beautiful plantation or grove of cypresses, ending in a covered terrace, from which there is a magnificent view over Genoa and the sea, and of the Riviera mountains, both east and west. Here is placed the image of the Immaculate Conception, mentioned at the opening of this chapter. According to an inscription on a square of marble underneath, an indulgence of forty days was granted by a bishop in 1842, to the devout recitation of an Ave Maria before this image. Walled off from the rest is a third garden, laid out chiefly in flower beds, with a summer-house at the farther end, containing a statue, large as life, of the Virgin, and another of a man kneeling before her at prayer. On the walls of the garden are several roughly executed fresco paintings.

The "Presepio" must not be passed over without a few words of description, although it is difficult to convey by words any accurate idea of the pretty and curious sight it presents to the eye. It is the custom in many Italian convents at Christmas to make a sort of representation of the Mysteries of the Nativity, by means of prettily-devised scenery and beautiful little figures, from one to two or three feet in height, and this religious show is called the " Presepio" or "Manger." The Presepio is erected annually at San Barnaba in a building of considerable size just outside the convent, and used only for this purpose. It is arranged in the form of a small theatre, one part forming a kind of stage, and the other occupied by the people, for whom *prie-dieus* are provided instead of benches. The main subject represented in this dramatic exhibition at San Barnaba was the adoration of the Magi. Mary, who was sitting in a rocky cave with the infant Jesus in her lap, was dressed in a gay-coloured robe, with a crown upon her head. The three Kings were arrayed in satin and gold, and followed by their train-bearers, banner-bearers, and other attendants; a little behind the Kings were their three palfreys, caparisoned in a stately manner. A star (made of gilt paper) shone brightly over the manger, and a ray of light extended from it directly upon the little Christ, whom angels were adoring from above. In the background were shepherds feeding their sheep The remainder of this religious spectacle was taken up by picturesque groups of men and women in every variety of gay costume, each in a different attitude, and with a different expression of countenance, announcing to one another the glad tidings of the Saviour's birth. In the distance were painted mountains, castles, and houses. The effect was increased by a curious optical illusion produced by rural scenery painted in fresco on the walls of the garden behind the Presepio, and seen through windows at the back of the latter. The Presepio is opened on Christmas night during the Midnight Mass and remains open, I believe, till Candlemas.

The community at San Barnaba at the period of my visit numbered twelve or thirteen friars, of whom four were lay-brothers, the remainder being in priest's orders. I will now describe briefly the ordinary method of life pursued by this religious fraternity. To begin with the matter of diet. They are at all times very spare in this respect; but during Lent, the self-denial practised at the Convent of San Barnaba is

extreme, as in addition to the fact that the
quantity of food taken is but small, they do not
eat meat, eggs, cheese, milk or butter. It
should be added, however, that this convent of
San Barnaba being the " Novizinto" or Novitiate,
for the reception and instruction of all the
novices of the Capuchin Order throughout the
province of Genoa, the discipline, especially in
the matter of fasting, is more rigid than in
other convents of the same Order.* In the
latter, a little meat and eggs are permitted on
certain days in Lent. The observance of three
Lents is common to the whole Order; but there
is this difference between the " Gran Cuaresima,"
the Great Lent, and the two extra Lents, that
in the latter, fasting is not obligatory on the
friars except in regard to the common meals in
the refectory. At the remaining seasons of the
year they eat meat, though in very small quantity, five times a week.

* There were not any novices at the convent at the
period of which I am writing, but when I visited
Genoa in the following year, there were at S. Barnaba
several of these close-shaven, meek-looking, youthful
postulants for the monastic habit.

Their dinner, which they usually take at a quarter past eleven, generally consists of a "minestra" or soup, almost always *maigre*, a small portion of meat, and a dish of vegetables or occasionally a very plain version of *omelette-aux-herbes*. They are allowed an ample portion of bread, and their beverage is wine and water ready mixed. At supper, out of Lent, they have a light "minestra," and one additional dish. In Lent, as well as on other fasting days, they do not take "cena" or supper, but "colezione" only, consisting of a small allowance of bread and vegetables. Before and after dinner and supper they stand in the middle of the refectory and recite a rather long Latin grace. No conversation is permitted during meals, a devotional book being read aloud. In the morning, early, they take a cup of coffee and a piece of bread, which latter, on fast days is limited to a mere mouthful, "per lo stomaco," for the stomach, as they say, but many do not avail themselves of this privilege, not breaking their fast until dinner.

The religious exercises performed by these friars are mainly as follows. As a general rule,

P

they rise to matins at midnight, the church bell being tolled the same at that hour as for the services in the day time.

"Slow o'er the midnight wave it swung."*

Less than ten minutes elapsed between the first sounding of the matin bell, and the commencement of the service. When therefore I attended the midnight Office, I was often unable to dress quickly enough to arrive before it had begun, so that as I threaded my way along the corridors, the distant hum of the friars' voices intoning matins would break on the ear. This circumstance, together with the fact of my being occasionally aided in finding my way through the silent and dimly-lighted passages by the beams of the "midnight moon" shining over the neighbouring sea, would recall to my mind these pretty lines of Scott:

"And when the midnight moon should lave
  Her forehead in the silver wave,
  How solemn on the ear would come,
  The holy matin's distant hum."†

They remained in choir at night for about an

* Marmion, canto 2.
† Lady of the Lake, canto 1.

hour and a half, for when matins and lauds were ended, the "Litany of the Saints" was recited, after which a short instruction was read from a book, and in conclusion followed private meditation. At six the friars,

"Roused by the crowing cock at dawn of day,"*

again repaired to the church for Prime, which was succeeded by Tierce and Sext, "Rosary of the Virgin," and meditation. The last and principal mass of the day, called the "conventual mass," was celebrated at seven, in presence of the whole fraternity. At eleven o'clock None was recited; and Vespers at some time in the afternoon, according to the season of the year, except during Lent when they are always recited before dinner. Complin was said in the evening, an hour before sunset, and at its termination followed "Litany of the Madonna," an instruction from a book, and meditation, after which a blessing was pronounced by the Superior, accompanied by sprinkling of holy water—all terminating at the Ave Maria, or sunset. After supper they went into the choir again for a short meditation before going to bed, but this

* Wordsworth.

was not obligatory, each friar performing this final act of devotion individually when it suited his convenience, and not in community.

The brotherhood at San Barnaba used the "discipline," or self-flagellation, four times a week in choir, the lamps being extinguished and the shutters shut during the process. This exercise has a very peculiar effect, being performed in complete darkness, and the infliction of the "discipline" causing a loud noise, such as would be made by a number of whips struck vigorously and continuously against some object, rendering it difficult to distinguish the words of the Miserere (or 51st psalm) which is recited during the flagellation. The "discipline" is used three times a week in Capuchin convents generally, but here it was administered a fourth time "per devozione alla Madonna," from devotion to the Madonna, the day selected for this supererogatory act of penance being Saturday, regarded by the Catholic Church as sacred to the Virgin Mary.

The government of the convent is directed by a Superior, who in this, as in the Franciscan Orders generally, is styled "Padre Guardiano;"

and second to him in authority is his deputy, the "Padre Vicario." As has been mentioned in describing the convent of La Concezione at Rome, the immediate Superior to the Guardian is the Provincial, who is the governor-general of all Capuchins within his province. San Barnaba is in the province of Genoa, comprising some thirty-two or thirty-three Capuchin monasteries. The Provincial resides at the Capo Convento or head-house of the province, situated in Genoa. He is subject to the General of the Order at Rome, with whom he is in frequent communication. The General is elected at a Chapter of the whole Order, held once in six years at Rome, and the Provincial of every province, and the Guardian of each convent, are elected by a provincial Chapter held triennially at the head-house of the province.

Besides the Superior, (whatever may be his title) and the Vicar of a monastery, there are several other officers of various degrees. The principal of these is the Padre Procuratore, or Proveditore, who acts as a kind of a steward of the temporalities of the convent, going to market to purchase provisions for the use of the monks, keeping the stores, &c. Another officer is the Sacristan, who has entire charge of the church, as well as of the ecclesiastical vestments. In large communities there is often more than one Sacristan, the senior in that case being in priest's orders. Then there are the Porter, (portinaio) and the Head-gardener, (ortolano), who are lay-brothers. And in convents of Mendicant Friars, several of the lay-brothers bear the name of Quæstors, (questori), their duty being to beg alms for the brotherhood. And lastly there is the Fra Cuoco—the convent cook—whose office is found to be as indispensable in the domestic economy of monasteries, as in that of more mundane establishments.

The convent of San Barnaba originally belonged to Cistercian nuns, but subsequently came into the possession of Dominican friars, from whom it was purchased for Capuchins, who have been here uninterruptedly since 1538, with the exception of eight years, (1810—1818) when the convent was closed, in common with the other convents of Italy, as one of the consequences of Napoleon's conquest. A document belonging to San Barnaba records that this general closing of the monasteries lasted from 1810 to 1815, but that owing to the dilapidated state of this convent, and the repairs which on that account were necessary, it was not re-opened until three years later. The same record informs us that it was for a time the "capo-convento," or head-convent of the Capuchins of the Province of Genoa, having been so created by Pope Paul III, in 1538. The instrument of this creation, which is extant, although I did not see it, requires that the Guardian shall annually offer a bouquet of flowers in the chapel of St. Catherine of Genoa. The interesting record from which I have derived these few facts, contains a list of all the Guardians or Superiors of the convent from 1538 to the present time. The list comprises the names of one hundred and six Superiors, it being the rule of the Order that the Guardian shall be changed every three years. The year in which each of them assumed the government is also given. While on the subject of the historical reminiscences connected with the convent of San Barnaba, I will insert copies of two inscriptions of considerable antiquarian interest, one of which I took from over the church door, and the second from over the gateway into the convent itself. The first is as follows:

> "†MCCLXXXVI Dna Leonora
> VSVS Maria Abbatissa
> Mouasterii Sci Barnabæ
> De Carbonaria Fecit
> Fieri hoc opus."*

Thus it appears that this monastery has existed for at least six centuries, that it flourished before some of our finest English cathedrals were built, and before the foundations were laid of many of those fine old abbeys in England, which have been tenantless ruins for centuries. Ages ago, when these abbeys, such as Bolton, Tintern, or Netley, were in the zenith of their prosperity, San Barnaba, too, was a flourishing monastery, and continues to be so to this day.†

* "Anno Domini twelve hundred and eighty-six, Mistress Leonora VSVS Maris (a latinized form of the lady's surname, the original of which is not known to the author), Abbess of the Monastery of St. Barnabas de Carbonaria caused this work to be done."

† Happening one day to be examining this inscrip-

The following is a copy of the second inscription:

" †MCCCLXII Die xv mensis Novembris
Reparatum fuit hoc monasterium tempore
——— Ciriance Bestagnæ abbatissæ hujus monasterii S. Barnabæ et postremò Añ Dñi MDCXXI
Die xv Augusti Lapis iste positus est."*

I am indebted to a friend, an intelligent Carmelite Friar of the Monastery of San Carlo at Genoa, Padre B——, for the suggestion that in the former inscription the words " VSVS Maris " are a latinized form of the name of the family to which the Abbess Leonora belonged, and which still exists, he said, as one of the noble families of Genoa; also for the information in company with a friar of the convent, I remarked on the large number of men and women who must have lived within its walls during the course of so many centuries, to which, after a moment's thought, the friar added emphatically, " E quanti Santi!" ("and how many saints among the number!").

* " A.D. thirteen hundred and sixty-two on the 15th day of the month of November, this monastery was repaired, in the time of ——— Ciriana Bestagna, Abbess of this Monastery of St. Barnabas, and lastly A.D. sixteen hundred and twenty-one, on the 15th day of August, this stone was placed here."

tion that the expression "De Carbonaria" refers to the old gateway by which you leave Genoa in ascending the mountain to San Barnaba, for though well acquainted with the gate itself, I had not before heard it called by that name. And lastly, the same friend offered the ingenious suggestion that the blank in this inscription probably contained some title, such as "Dominæ," before the name of the Abbess, for the blank appears to have been made by an intentional and recent erasure, according with the fact, (which I state on the authority of my informant) that Napoleon during his rule in Italy, caused all titles in public inscriptions to be erased.

I confess I felt great interest in studying this monastic life and its various incidents, and the more so considering to how few persons such an opportunity of studying it thus minutely has been afforded. Most English people regard Monasticism as so essentially mediæval, so entirely a thing of the past, that it seemed strange to see in such minute detail all the essentials and concomitants of monastic life in daily practice; and this, too, not in a newly built convent professedly constructed to carry out some pre-conceived theory of mediæval monachism, but in a monastery which has existed for six hundred years, as inscriptions and other records testify. Whether we consider the long choral offices, the severe fasts, the use of the "discipline," the appearance and manners of the friars, and their retired regular life; or the convent itself, with its dormitories and cells, cloisters and refectory, church and choir, &c., we have here a complete type of a monastery and of monastic life. I was particularly interested in the choral services, and when I attended in choir, and heard the friars of San Barnaba recite the Breviary, my thoughts were carried back to the series of centuries during which the same offices have been said regularly in the same little choir, and by similar quaint-looking monks.

Among many matters, some of them apparently slight and unimportant, though tending in the aggregate to convey an idea of the actual monastic life of the present day in Italy, I will, before concluding this chapter, note down a few miscellaneous facts connected with my conventual experiences.

It happened on one occasion that the clerk, whose duty it was to rouse the community for matins, overslept himself, in consequence of which matins instead of being said at midnight, were deferred until an hour or two before the ordinary hour of Prime. A friar happened to observe to me that if this was repeated it would probably be visited with some penalty. I inquired what kind of penalty would be resorted to, to which he replied, perhaps the loss of the offending brother's " pictanza," or pittance,* an expression which, though meaning literally his scanty conventual commons, seems to be used to signify the principal dish at dinner, generally (when not a fast day) a very limited allowance of meat. I may add that the clerk in question had in his cell a small clock

* This reminds me of a curious charter of Robert I, King of Scotland, to the Abbey of Melross, called 'Carta de Pitancia Centum Librarum,' from which I make the subjoined extract. It would appear, by the way, that "rice milk" was as common and homely a dish in those times as it is at the present day. "Carta Regis Roberti I, Abbati et Conventui de Melross. —— singulis diebus cuilibet monacho monasterii predicti comedenti in refectorio unum sufficiens ferculum risa-

with an alarum, which was set at about midnight to awake him for matins. This clerk, Fra G——, was then a sub-deacon, and studying for priest's orders. He told me that he had already been studying two years and a quarter, and had to continue his studies for another four years or more. He also informed me that he had embraced the monastic state by the advice of his two elder brothers, both of whom were friars, and who (as well as himself) were greatly pleased with this method of life. He was, I believe, twenty-one years of age, and seemed happy and cheerful. He always remained within the convent enclosure, dividing his time between his clerical studies, and the duties of Sucristan of the church, which devolved upon him.

Whenever the friars go in or out of choir, they kneel down and kiss the floor in token of humility. In the choir is a sort of clock, which, when wound up, goes for an hour, striking at

rum factarum cum lacte, amigdalarum vel pisarum [*sic*] sive aliorum ciborum consimilis condicionis inventorum in patria, et illud ferculum ferculum Regis vocabitur in æternum."

each quarter, and which is used to regulate the time devoted to meditation. At four different periods during the twenty-four hours of every day do the Capuchins here meditate together in choir in complete silence, viz., early in the morning, between six and seven; in the afternoon, after complin; for a short time after supper, before going to bed; and after matins. The convent gates are closed, barred, and locked for the night at the Ave Maria, or sunset.

San Barnaba, like convents generally, is in every part full of signs and memorials of religion. Crucifixes and crosses, images, paintings, and devotional inscriptions abound everywhere. The inscriptions for the most part recommend the virtue of silence. Written up in large letters in the dormitories are the following: "Silentium;" "Religiosus si silentiosus;" and "Religionis silentium clavis." Outside the convent gate is a little building, where the friars receive their lady relations; for no woman can, under any pretext, be admitted, except in the rare case of her having obtained a Brief from the Pope authorizing her admission. The lay-brothers go out frequently to beg alms, generally in kind, one day being appropriated to begging bread, another for wine, a third for oil, and so on. This convent has a curious agreement with the great Capuchin convent at Genoa, by which in consideration of a stipulated sum of money paid by the latter, the community of San Barnaba abstain from begging alms within the city of Genoa, thus avoiding the possibility of the two religious fraternities interfering with one another.

The friars when they go out to beg alms in kind, carry a large white linen bag or wallet, in which their benefactors place bread, cheese, and other provisions. When these bags become filled, and therefore heavy, the begging friar will often throw it across his shoulder, as frequently represented in pictures. During my stay at San Barnaba I have occasionally seen Fra G———, the lay-brother appointed to beg alms for the community, (the "questori" are always lay-brothers), at work with his needle and thread in the cloister or convent garden, mending his wallet.

During my sojourn at this and other convents, I had an opportunity of observing the great importance that is attached in Italy to the practice of auricular confession, as an essential part of religion by both clergy and laity, and the safeguards by which it is sought to protect that practice from abuse. Although a priest by virtue of his ordination becomes *ipso facto*, competent to hear confessions, it is nevertheless contrary to ecclesiastical discipline for him to do so unless specially licensed for that purpose by the bishop of the diocese, if he be a secular priest, or by the Provincial, if a member of a religious order. And even of those clergymen who are licensed to hear confessions, it is not by any means all who are permitted to confess women, a special faculty being required for that purpose. These limitations in regard to confessions are especially frequent in convents, where the number of persons in priest's orders is considerable, rendering it practicable to make a selection of those most suited for the duties of confession. At San Barnaba, whilst I was there, only two of the friars used to hear the confessions of women—the Superior and another. On one occasion when I was walking in the cloister, the bell of the convent gate rang several times without being answered. I therefore opened the gate, and found an old woman waiting, who in reply to a question from me, said she desired to speak to "quello che confessa le donne,"* meaning a particular friar, though she did not mention his name. The description was, however, sufficiently intelligible to enable me to send to her the confessor she wished to see. *Apropos* of confessors, on another occasion, when talking to some ladies near the Church of San Barnaba, a Capuchin friar passed by, whereupon three of the young ladies and their brother hastened to salute him, each of them successively seizing his hand and kissing it. They afterwards told me that this friar had formerly been their confessor, and, added one of the younger ladies laughingly, " sa tutti i nostri segreti !" (he knows all our secrets).

It is a fact not without interest, that in the small library of the little rural convent of San Barnaba, I met with a copy of Young's Night Thoughts, with the English original on one page, and a French translation on the opposite side. I had never before, as it happened, read

* He who hears the confessions of women.

this book, and it certainly seemed an odd coincidence that led me to find such a work in an Italian monastery, and to read it there for the first time.

I will conclude this sketch of the Convent of San Barnaba, and of the life led within its walls, by referring to the rhymes, "le rime," which were improvised by one of the friars at the mid-day meal in the refectory on Easter Sunday. I have often observed the general cheerfulness prevailing among members of religious communities. San Barnaba was an instance of this, although a more than usually rigid convent (being the novitiate house) of an unusually strict Order. On Easter day, after the religious duties of the morning had been performed, and after the Paschal lamb had been blessed, as is customary in convents, the Superior dispensed with the public reading during dinner in honour of the festival of Easter, and the friars enjoyed the privilege of conversing whilst taking their meal. There was a good deal of quiet conversation, and towards the end of dinner one of the friars—a stout elderly lay-brother of small stature and ruddy complexion, who had passed the greater part of his monastic life of thirty odd years in this convent—was asked by his Superior to improvise some lines for the amusement of the company. The lay-brother requested to be furnished with a subject, to which the Superior replied by suggesting the name of their guest, for the purpose. This was a rather unpromising subject for the good friar, who however made the most he could of it; for rising at once and bowing respectfully to the Superior, he improvised several lines, which whatever may have been their merit, served for the great amusement of his hearers, whose simple and hearty merriment on such slight grounds it was pleasant both to see and to share in.

CHAPTER XI.

Carnival at Genoa—Visits to Religious Houses at and near Genoa.

Soon after my arrival at San Barnaba, I had the opportunity of seeing the celebration of the Carnival at Genoa, which, however, is a very small affair, compared with that of Rome. Among the principal Carnival days at Genoa is the Thursday before Ash Wednesday, called "Giovedi Grasso," from its festive character. At an early hour in the afternoon the shops were closed, and the streets—especially the Strada Carlo Felice, the Via Nuova and Nuovissima, and other chief thoroughfares—soon became thronged by masses of people. I cannot call them sight-seers, for there was scarcely anything to see, the wearers of dominoes being few and far between, and walking through the crowd in a most orderly way, without playing off tricks as they do at Rome and elsewhere.

CARNIVAL AT GENOA.

The great amusement of the multitude seemed to consist in the feeling that the day was a holyday, and that they were promenading among such a mass of their fellow creatures. The occasional passing of a few dominoes added an element of fun and gaiety to the scene. In the evening, at all the theatres *bals masqués* were given in honour of the Carnival.

Giovedi Grasso is observed even in convents by a "pranzo" or dinner, somewhat more liberal than usual. I had the good fortune (which rarely happens to laymen) of being invited to dine with my monastic friends at San Bartolommeo,[*] "per far Carnivale con loro," as the Superior jokingly said when giving the invitation. It felt strange to go out to dinner at noon, and to take leave of one's hosts within little more than an hour afterwards. And yet

[*] As an illustration of the small intercourse that exists between members of different religious Orders, I may mention that none of the friars of San Barnaba (where I was now staying) knew, or were known to, any of the Barnabites at San Bartolommeo degli Armeni, although of course the names and situations of their respective convents were well known to both.

I do not know that I ever enjoyed an invitation more thoroughly.*

The following Sunday also is a great Carnival day, but on this occasion torrents of rain interfered with its celebration. This *contretemps* was, however, compensated for on Shrove Tuesday, when the vast masses of people by whom the streets were thronged, was in itself a sight to see. It seemed as if every man, woman and child had turned out to join in the holyday-making. The dominoes were more numerous than on previous days, and in the evening the *bals masqués* were repeated.

On the next morning, Ash Wednesday, the solemn fast of Lent began. At the Convent of San Barnaba where I was staying, the ceremony of blessing the ashes was performed before the principal mass of the day, after which every-

---

* "I proposed to take up my quarters at the convent for a few days; and I know no pleasanter place where a man disposed to take the world as it goes could spend his time. . . . He has the variety of a large household without the bustle of an inn; the cheerfulness of a table-d'hôte free from the vulgarity of" a "travelling mob; . . and the society of a body of gentlemen, &c."—*Tales of the Great St. Bernard.*

body present approached the altar rails, and kneeling down, the officiating priest signed their foreheads with ashes in the form of a cross saying at the same time, "Memento, homo, ut pulvis es, et in pulverem reverteris,"— Remember, man, that thou art dust, and to dust thou shalt return. Hence the origin of the name "Ash Wednesday." This ceremony in the language of the Roman Church, is called a "sacramental," partaking, that is, in some degree of sacramental efficacy, although not actually a sacrament.

In the course of my stay at San Barnaba I visited several religious houses at and near Genoa, which I had not seen during my visit of the previous year. Among the number, at a short distance from Genoa on the east side, was the large and handsome Convent of "Riformati" or Recollects, called "il Monte," from its position on a lofty hill, commanding perhaps the finest view at Genoa. The convent was shewn to me by an intelligent friar named Padre Vincenzo, who, although not young, appeared a picture of health and spirits. He told me he had been professed upwards of thirty years. The community consisted of thirty friars, of whom twenty-two were in priest's orders, and eight lay-brothers. My informant confirmed what I had heard before, that the Recollects rise to matins at midnight. They are, as has been mentioned in a previous chapter, one of the branches of the Franciscan Order. Their dress is very similar to that worn by the Capuchins, but the fact of the Recollects not wearing any beard, makes a great difference in their appearance. A thick wood, called "Bosco" in Italian, is attached to the monastery, and contributes much to the charms of this pleasant retreat. At regular intervals along the winding path leading up the steep hill to the convent, is a series of small square chapels each in honour of one of the fourteen "stations of the cross," a devotion in memory of the several parts of Christ's Passion.

A few days later, I visited a convent of Augustinian nuns. I was of course only able to enter the church of the nunnery, and to converse for a few moments with the portress, a lay-sister, to whom I had been introduced previously by a priest. This convent is situated on the mountains behind Genoa, near the monastery of La Madonnetta, belonging to Austin Friars. The nun told me she had been in that convent for thirty-nine years, having come as a pupil when twelve years old, and having taken the vows at eighteen.

> "She early took the veil and hood,
> Ere upon life she cast a look,
> Or knew the world that she forsook.
> Love, to her ear, was but a name,
> Combined with vanity and shame;
> Her hopes, her fears, her joys, were all
> Bounded within the cloister wall."*

She said there were ten choir sisters, exclusive of the lay-sisters; that the Superior is styled "Madre Superiore," or "Madre" only; and that they do not on ordinary occasions recite the seven canonical hours daily, or as she termed it, the "uficio della chiesa universale," but the Office of the Madonna only. She added that this is not properly a "monastero," but a "conservatorio," the difference, as she explained it, being that the latter is subject to the jurisdiction of the bishop of the diocese, instead of to

* Marmion.

the General of the Order, like a "monastero" strictly so called. The cheerful manner of this Augustinian nun recalled to my mind Wordsworth's couplet:

"Nuns fret not at their convent's narrow room,
And hermits are contented with their cells."

As I descended the mountain in returning from the nunnery, I went over a monastery of Austin Friars, called San Nicola. These Barefooted Augustinians have also the appellation of Hermits of St. Austin. I was shewn over San Nicola, which is a large and rather handsome convent internally, by Fra Silvestro, who told me that the novitiate in that Order is of four years' duration, and that he himself was then a novice, but expected to take the vows in the following June, when he would have completed his fourth year of probation. "Son' ancora libero," (I am still free) he said. In answer to my inquiry whether he had made up his mind to become a professed monk, and whether he looked forward with pleasure to doing so, he replied to both questions decidedly in the affirmative. I regret to say that this long novitiate appears to be quite an exceptional thing in the monastic system; the reply in other cases in which I have asked the length of the novitiate being in nearly every instance, "un anno." The Superior in this Order is styled Prior, and the friars exchange their own names for the name of some favourite saint, as is the case with the Cistercians, Franciscans, Carmelites, and most of the older religious Orders. On the other hand, many comparatively modern Orders retain their own christian and surnames, examples of which may be found in the Jesuits, Barnabites, Scolopi, &c.

The Padri Scolopi are one of the most interesting of the religious Orders that devote themselves to works of charity. The object of their institute is to give gratuitous instruction in nearly every branch of learning, from the most elementary to the most advanced. Hence their name of Scolopi, a contraction of "scuole pie," or "pious schools." Padre Massa, of the Scolopi convent at Genoa, informed me that at that convent they give instruction wholly gratuitous to seven hundred pupils, divided into various classes according to the subjects to be studied. He said that not only the poor attend, but many persons of the highest families in Genoa, all of whom are taught together without distinction of rank. The religious community there numbers about fifteen. I saw one or two of the classes being taught by the Padri. Padre Massa told me that the Scolopi had eight houses in the Sardinian States, and many in the Neapolitan and Papal dominions, including three at Rome. The Order was founded under the name of the "Pious Schools of the Mother of God," in the year 1621, by St. Joseph Calasanctius, a native of Arragon. The Superior of each community is styled Padre Rettore.

The Padri Crociferi, or Cross-bearers, the last of the monastic Orders that I visited at Genoa, have a pretty church and convent nearly opposite the hospital. Their name is derived from a red cross they wear on their cassock. The special function of the Crociferi is to attend on the sick. Neither they nor the Scolopi were included in the law for the suppression of the monasteries in the Sardinian dominions passed a few years ago. The community here consisted of fourteen persons, including the lay-brothers. The Superior has the title of Padre Prefetto.

The Padri Crociferi, as well as the corresponding Order of nuns, were founded by St. Camillus de Lellis, towards the close of the sixteenth century.

The two last named Orders, the Scolopi and the Crociferi, belong to that branch of the monastic body called Regular Clerks. Among the other principal congregations of Regular Clerks are the Theatins, instituted by St. Cajetan in 1524; the Barnabites, founded at Milan in 1533; the Jesuits, instituted in 1540; the Somaschi, founded by St. Jerome Emilian at Somascha, a village near Milan, in 1530; Regular Clerks, called Minors, founded in 1588; and Regular Clerks of the Mother of God, instituted at Lucca in 1628.* Each of these Orders is devoted to some active work of charity, the majority of them being engaged in tuition. They are nevertheless strictly monastic bodies, living in convents according to a fixed rule, and with regular conventual discipline. They are regarded as belonging as much to the regular

* There are several other Orders, some or all of which, I believe, belong to the Regular Clerks, such as the Servites, Gerolimini, Redemptorists and Rosminiani.

clergy, (or monks) as the Benedictines, or Franciscans, in which respect they differ from the several congregations of *secular* priests, such as the Oratorians and Lazarists, who, (although they, too, live in convents, according to monastic rule and discipline, and on that account have the monastic title of "Padre") are considered to be still secular priests, because they do not take perpetual vows, and consequently cannot be considered to have permanently "renounced the world."

These congregations of priests, both regular and secular, possess in common the characteristic of combining external duties, either of tuition, preaching, or ministering to the sick, with conventual life. They had their origin, for the most part, contemporaneously with the Reformation, having been generally founded with the object of checking the spread of the Reformed doctrines, by educating the laity in accordance with the tenets of the old faith.

CHAPTER XII.

Excursion to the Convent of Campi.

ON the afternoon of the first Sunday in March I set out on a short excursion to a monastery named Campi, about five miles from Genoa, where I hoped to pass one or two days, being provided with a letter of introduction from the Superior of San Barnaba. The latter was preaching the Lent at a village some three miles off, named Premontone, and as it lay at no great distance out of the road to Campi, I determined to go round by that way and hear the sermon. I thought it would be a good opportunity of seeing Italian village life on a Sunday.

Accompanied by the Fra Cuoco—the monastic cook—of San Barnaba, who happened to be going to Premontone, I left Genoa by its western extremity, after ascending the steep hill leading to the Porta degli Angeli (if I remember rightly the name), a little beyond which, on an equally elevated position, stand the parish and church of Premontone. It was three in the afternoon, and the tolling of the church bell announced the approaching service. Groups of rustics were assembled here and there in holyday attire near the church door, conversing together until the sound of the bell should cease. Entering the church, I found it quite filled by country people. Marked simplicity and neatness were the main characteristics of the building. The preacher—the Superior of San Barnaba—soon appeared in the pulpit. He stood before you, a venerable old man, with shaven head and long white beard. He wore the brown serge habit of his Order, with a knotted cord hanging from his waist, and sandals on his feet. Facing him, on the pulpit desk, was a tall image of the crucified Saviour. Here was presented to the eye a complete realization of the Italian preacher and monk. This friar, in whose countenance the traits of habitual self-denial were mingled with a smile peculiarly sweet, harangued his hearers in glowing language, and with gestures suited to the word, exhorting them to penance and mortification.* Leading a life of retirement and self-denial himself, he seemed entitled to preach self-denial to others. His very aspect, coupled with the high estimation in which he was held, was itself a speaking sermon. If there are sermons in stones, there are sermons also in *men*. The service concluded with the "Benediction of the Sacrament," in which, after some hymns and a prayer or two, the priest blessed the people, making the sign of the cross over them with the Host, which (enclosed in a gilt case or remonstrance) he held in his hands.

After service I was introduced by the Superior of San Barnaba to the "Parroco," or parish-priest of Premontone, in the adjoining parsonage, called in Italian Canonica, which was a small unpretending cottage. And yet, to my surprise, in this rural parsonage I found an excellent library. Among the books with which the shelves were laden, my eye fell upon a handsome edition of Fleury's Ecclesiastical History, several volumes of Rollin's Belles Lettres, fine folio editions of St. Chrysostom,

* Addison, in the 'Spectator,' gives an interesting description of the fervid eloquence, and enthusiastic manner of Italian preachers in his day.

of St. Gregory Nazianzen, and other Fathers, an Italian version of Ossian's Poems, and many valuable works in addition. The "Parroco" himself was a tall, slender grey-haired man of dignified appearance. After partaking of a glass of wine which the clergyman offered me, I resumed my way to Campi, under the guidance of a sweet-faced child whom he insisted on sending with me. Indeed so circuitous was the route—up and down a succession of hills, and along steep rough paths—that I should not easily have found the road alone. When, on arriving at the convent gate, I gave the boy a small piece of silver for his trouble, he seemed delighted beyond measure, and smiling, exclaimed "Ma è troppo !"—"It is too much."

Campi is the name of a large convent situated half way up the side of one of the range of hills forming the well-known valley of Polcevera, by which Genoa is approached from Turin. Coming from Turin it is on the right hand side shortly before arriving at San Pierre d'Arena. The convent is dedicated to the Virgin and takes its name from the biblical words, "Ego flos campi, et lilium convallium," —"I am the flower of the field, and the lily of the valleys," (Book of Canticles)—which are applied by the Roman Church to the mother of Christ. The situation of this convent, and the approach to it, are as pretty as its poetical name. Ascending the hill gradually from the valley of Polcevera you see the large pile of buildings stretched along the side of the hill, and commanding a delightful view. The entrance to the convent is strikingly picturesque, with a charming piazza in front, containing a large wooden cross and several elegant cypresses. This is one of the handsomest Capuchin monasteries I know. It had been much enlarged within the last twenty years by the late Marquis Pallavincini, a Genoese noble. The church and choir, the cloister, the refectory, the dormitories, the spacious library, the extensive gardens, and the pleasant "bosco" or wood, together with the good friars themselves, were full of interest to me. The view from the library windows, and from the garden, over the valley of Polcevera and the Mediterranean beyond, is most lovely.

On the morning after my arrival, I visited an Abbey of Regular Canons of St. John Lateran, also called of St. Austin, built on the summit of the same hill on the side of which is the Convent of Campi, which latter therefore the abbey overlooks. I was much interested in this monastery, called Nostra Signora della Coronata, both because I had not before visited any house of that Order, and because Thomas à Kempis, the author of several admirable devotional works,* and the reputed author of the incomparable treatise, "De Imitatione Christi," was a Regular Canon of St. Austin. I brought with me no introduction, but nevertheless soon made friends with one or two of the canons, especially the Canonico Schiafini, who was zealous in supporting the claims of A Kempis to the authorship of the "Imitation of Christ." He was kind enough to lend me a Latin essay to solve the doubts I expressed on the subject. It made out a good *primâ facie* case on behalf of its hero, but was altogether *ex parte*, not professing to give the other side of the question, which has been advocated by many high authorities. The Austin Canons† are popularly

---

* The principal of the undisputed works of Thomas à Kempis, are the 'Soliloquium Animæ,' the 'Vallis Liliorum,' and the 'Hortulus Rosarum,' each of which is an excellent specimen of the devotional literature of the Middle Ages.

† Among the Houses of Austin Canons in England at the Reformation, was one in the parish of Tandridge, Surrey, called Tandridge Priory, and dedicated to St. James. It was founded in the reign of Richard I,

called Rocchettini, from the dress of the Order consisting of a "rocchetto," or short linen surplice worn over a white "sottana" or cassock; but on ordinary occasions they are often dressed in black. The abbot of this monastery of "La Coronata" is mitred and croziered, and his vicar, or second in authority, is styled Prior. The abbey church, although in so isolated a situation, is parochial, and the present prior—not the abbot—is the "parroco," or parish priest. The church is both spacious and handsome, and contains an image of the Virgin crowned in glory, said to be miraculous, whence the name of the abbey, La Coronata. I may mention, by the way, as a curious sign of the times, and as an odd mingling of the new with the old, that I saw posted up outside of the refectory door, a time-table of the Turin railway, which passes through the valley beneath. What a contrast in the current of ideas suggested, respectively, by a monastery—with its mediæval associations—and a railway—the very type of modern go-ahead progress ! I was informed that the "abate" has sometimes occasion to go to Turin on business, which was the reason of the time-table being there.

and suppressed in 1537 (or in the preceding year) when its income was valued at £86 7s 6d.

At a stone's throw from the abbey, and dependent on it, is a large Oratory, which Canonico Schiafini was kind enough to take me to see; and I may say it equally delighted and surprised me. The oratory is a chapel of great size, decorated with so much taste and liberality, and even splendour, that you would suppose it was rather a royal chapel than a simple oratory placed on a mountain top. The entire roof and walls are very elegantly painted, and the floor is formed throughout of coloured marbles. This chapel is also enriched with good easel paintings.

I made a second visit to the Abbey of La Coronata on the following day. On my way up the hill to the abbey, I met a grey-haired ecclesiastic dressed in a white cassock and short linen surplice, over which he wore a black cloak. Believing him to be the abbot, I addressed him as such, and he proved to be so. We conversed for some minutes, during which he mentioned that there is more than one branch of the Regular Canons of St. Austin, and also expressed his regret that Thomas à Kempis had never been canonised.

Whilst walking in the abbey cloister, I was joined by the Canonico Schiafini, with whom I was glad to enter into conversation. He told me, *inter alia*, that the General of the Order nominates the "parroco," who however owes obedience to the Archbishop of Genoa in strictly parochial matters; also, that mitred abbots do not wear the "mitra preciosa," but the "mitra simplex," (or plain white mitre) only, and that they are restricted in performing service pontifically, (that is with episcopal ceremonial) to three times a year. On taking leave of the Canonico, I walked along the hills beyond the abbey as far as a wood, at the beginning of which is a tiny chapel, a *cappellina*, with a picture representing Christ bearing his cross, whence you obtain a fine view of the mountains of the Riviera, westwards towards Nice.

In the Convent of Campi was a boy about eighteen or nineteen years of age, who went on errands, and assisted the lay-brothers generally in their household duties. While taking the usual cup of *caffè nero* one morning, I had a few minutes' conversation with this lad. He was unable to read, but when I mentioned the subject of religion he became quite animated, notwithstanding his ignorance of secular learning. He took out from his coat pocket two rosaries, one of which he called "della Madonna," and the other "del Signore, che," (he added with a sympathizing expression of countenance, which a painter would have been delighted to seize), "che ha tanto patito per noi altri, nel portando la croce al monte Calvario."* From another pocket he drew, wrapped up in a little bag, a small silver crucifix given to him by a friar, and to which he said an "indulgence" was attached by the recitation of a Paternoster. Then he showed me, fastened to his neck, two medals, to which also some indulgence was attached by saying five Paternosters. In answer to questions from me, he said that he repeated these prayers daily, and those of the two rosaries morning and evening. Speaking of the suppression of the monasteries, he exclaimed, "Ma che diverrebbe di noi peccatori, se i frati non pregavano per noi? Se non era per i Religiosi, il mondo caderebbe sotto il peccato. E stanno essi sempre in convento, e non fanno male a nessuno."† He regretted the suppression the more, as he said he had a

* "Who suffered so much for us in carrying the cross to Mount Calvary."

† "But what would become of us sinners if the friars did not pray for us? Were it not for the Religious, the world would fall beneath the weight of sin. And these remain always in their convents, and do injury to nobody."

vocation for a religious life, and wished to enter a monastery.

Although I came over here from San Barnaba, intending to stay only a single day, the Guardian pressed me so warmly to remain longer, that I felt equally compelled and pleased to prolong my visit for a few days. The beauty of the scenery, the prettiness of the convent itself, and the cordial though simple manners of the religious fraternity, all united to render my sojourn agreeable. It was a pleasure to rise at midnight to matins, than which service, at such an hour, nothing makes you enter more intimately into the spirit of monastic life ; and unless a person is competent to enter into that spirit, it is impossible to form a judgment approximating even to truth, in regard either to the favourable or unfavourable side of monastic institutions.

Among the friars was an old man of a strikingly venerable appearance, and much respected. He told me he had been in his youth a soldier in Napoleon's army, and on his discharge in 1814, entered the Capuchin Order, when twenty-four years of age, being then, he added, " già vecchio" (already old,) to commence a religious life. This remark is an illustration of the very early age at which it is usual for persons to bind themselves by monastic vows. Padre S— complained bitterly, at least if the mild accents in which a monk allows himself to complain can be so termed, of the injustice and despotism of the Government in forbidding the convents to take novices. He said this was a great hardship upon many who wished to adopt a monastic life, and contended that such a policy was wholly inconsistent with the liberty which was professedly the basis of the Constitution. He did not dwell upon the confiscation of the whole of the property of the Mendicant Orders of both sexes, without compensation even of the most nominal kind;* this, he added, could be borne with patience, but the forcible prohibition to enter those Orders was, he argued, altogether unjustifiable, especially in the case of a government founded on the principle of liberty.

I saw when at Campi an interesting statistical table of the Capuchin Order in the year 1775. There were then, it appears, upwards of 31,000 Capuchin friars and 1726 convents. Of these,

* The Endowed Orders, when suppressed, receive a small annuity, but the Mendicant Orders *nothing*—their scanty furniture and vestments, and even their little libraries, being turned into money for the benefit of the government.

6000 friars were in Naples and Sicily, more than 4000 in France, 3000 in Spain, 1800 in the Sardinian States, &c. I was surprised to observe that there were 14 Capuchin convents in Ireland at that time, containing 154 friars. This Order, in the year 1853, comprised 11,000 friars.

Before leaving Campi I made a visit to San Gaetano in San Pierre d'Arena, a succursal church (analogous to a "chapel of ease" in England) served by Regular Canons of St. Austin. Unlike most Italian churches, it has no fresco or other coloured decorations on the roof or walls, nor any marbles, but the interior nevertheless is very beautiful in point of architecture, being a fine specimen of Palladian. On the walls are elegant arabesques in stucco, and the columns and friezes are graceful. The same afternoon I walked to Raviolo, a village in the valley of Polcevera where I visited the suppressed Carthusian monastery, the cloisters of which are large and still handsome, although partly dilapidated and used for secular purposes. The church of the old monastery is now parochial and was shewn to me by the Parroco Oggiro, whose acquaintance I chanced to make when examining his church. He took me into the

Canonica or parsonage, where he insisted on my accepting a glass of excellent white wine. I observed several large ecclesiastical tomes in the room in which we sat. The Parroco told me that the Carthusians were expelled from this monastery in the revolution at Genoa in 1797; and that a few years since the Prior of the Certosa at Pavia came over to negotiate the repurchase of the old convent, but finding the expense of putting it into repair and of buying up land, &c., for securing the *clausura* too great, he relinquished the design.

The next day I took leave of Campi and its hospitable inmates. The Superior accompanied me to the convent gate, where, with many a bow accompanied by the usual " a rivederla" (*au revoir*) he bade me adieu. Before doing so, however, he had regaled me with some wine from Alicante, and also with *bonbons* which had been presented to him as their confessor by young girls on their marriage, or on taking the veil—a gift which, it seems, it is usual for them on such occasions to make to all their friends. In returning to my quiet retreat at San Barnaba, I stopped on the way to see the small Abbey of San Teodoro, belonging to Regular Canons of St. Austin, and giving name to the western suburb of Genoa, by which you approach the city in coming from Nice. The convent itself is not remarkable; but the church is pretty, and has a fine painting in the sanctuary. A number of children were assembled in the church, whom several priests were instructing. The cloister contained a Latin epitaph engraved upon a stone tablet on the wall, erected by the Regular Canons in the year 1483 to the memory of a benefactor of the convent. This is speaking evidence of the antiquity of the abbey, as well as of the length of time during which its present owners have been there. Previous to 1849, when the abbey was sacked during the revolution by the royal troops, the Abbot used to officiate pontifically twice a year with great ceremony; but all the vestments, &c., having then disappeared, the pontifical celebrations have since been discontinued. At the period of my visit it contained only four monks, viz., the Abbot, the Prior, (who is the Parroco, the abbey church being parochial), a third canon, and a lay-brother. It is to the politeness of this lay-brother, who conducted me over the convent, that I am indebted for these particulars.

CHAPTER XIII.

Pedestrian Tour to Convents on the Riviera.

BEFORE finally leaving Genoa, I made a short pedestrian tour along part of the Riviera. In addition to the beautiful scenery of that delightful sea-side route, I hoped to have the advantage of visiting a few country convents, to which I had been fortunate enough to obtain introductions. I accordingly set out on foot at seven o'clock on a morning in the middle of April, intending to walk to Voltri, on the Nice road the same day; but I had barely got as far as Sestri Ponente, only five miles from Genoa, when the rain descended in such torrents that it became impossible to proceed. I took shelter in the Monastery of San Martino, situated on an eminence behind Sestri, and, although unprovided with an introduction, the Vice-Principal (for the Guardian was away, having been preaching the Lent in some distant parish) received me most hospitably. I intended to have resumed my journey the same afternoon, but as the rain continued unabated during the whole of that and the following day, and I was pressed to remain till the weather should clear, my stay at San Martino extended over forty-eight hours. I had no cause to regret the inclemency of the season, for I enjoyed my sojourn there exceedingly.

San Martino is a pleasant little convent, having a pretty quadrangular cloister, with a nicely-cultivated garden in the centre of the quadrangle, containing four orange trees, then bearing ripe fruit; and on the roof of one of the four sides of the cloister is a charming terrace *al fresco*, with a fine view over the sea. The " Vicario," or Vice-Principal, informed me that, according to a current tradition, the Mediterranean had once reached up to this terrace, although at present the town of Sestri stands between it and and the sea. The walls of the cloister are enlivened by numerous small woodcuts of saints and others of reputed sanctity, with letterpress at foot giving a summary of the life and virtues of the persons represented above. In the wet and cold weather that prevailed during my sojourn at San Martino, I used frequently to take exercise in the cloister, stopping now and then to read some of these epitomised " Acta Sanctorum."

I dined with the community in the refectory at a quarter past eleven, and supped at the Ave Maria or sunset. I always enjoy a meal taken in a refectory. Indeed such are the circumstances, partly artistic and partly religious, by which such a meal is usually accompanied, that what is elsewhere so essentially a common-place affair, becomes associated in the case of a convent with sentiments of a moral kind. The artistic effect of a refectory—oblong in shape, with folding doors at one end and long narrow oak tables extending round the room, and pictures representing religious subjects suspended at intervals along the walls; combined with the formal Latin grace before and after meals, the spiritual reading, the frugal fare, and the quaint, picturesque appearance of the monks or friars themselves, all tend to impart a peculiar charm to a convent meal.

I left San Martino on a Friday morning at eight o'clock, having with difficulty prevailed on the Superior to accept a small *elemosina*, or alms, for the benefit of the convent in return for the hospitality I had enjoyed. I visited, in passing, the parish church of Sestri, which for so small a place is both large and handsome. After passing through several villages, of which Pegli was one, I reached Voltri, a flourishing town of about 8000 inhabitants. On the road thither was a temporary straw cabin wherein sat a blind man and a fine-looking boy, eight or ten years of age, both of them hatless and shoeless. The blind man was engaged in active conversation with the boy, and as I approached I could hear that he was catechising the child preparatory to his first communion. The latter made astonishingly long and rapid replies to some of the questions. One of these was, "Che è il vero pentimento?" "What is true repentance?" to which the boy answered, "Il dolore d'avere peccato, per puro amore di Dio," "Sorrow for sin, conceived from pure love of God." Interrogatories on the principal articles of faith followed, and as to the nature of "mortal sin," each of which he replied to with great readiness. The blind man told me that he, and also a brother of his, had both been blind from their birth.

Being tired by the walk, I was glad to repose for a few hours in the Convent of San Nicola, whose Superior I had met at San Barnaba. This convent is finely situated on a high point of the mountains behind Voltri, and the view from it, over the mountain peaks on the land side, and the Mediterranean on the other, is superb. According to a comparatively modern inscription which I read, the church of this convent was founded in A.D. 343, and consecrated A.D. 345. I recommenced my walk the same afternoon towards Varazze, a small town on the seaboard about thirteen miles distant. The first town after leaving Voltri is Arenzano. The bit of road between these two places is highly interesting, lying close upon the *marina*, or seaboard, with the blue sea on the left hand, and overhanging rocky cliffs on the right, the road winding perpetually so as to follow the indentations of the alternately projecting and receding shore. On quitting the pretty little town of Arenzano, the scenery becomes more varied, the road thence to Varazze running for the most part at a distance from the sea, and through some beautiful mountain valleys, especially one which you pass soon after quitting Arenzano. The abundance of wood, too, on the mountains of this part of the Riviera, adds greatly to the beauty of their effect.

I reached the convent at Varazze, to which I had an introduction, about dusk, and remained there till the following afternoon, enjoying much my stay within its peaceful walls. I supped that night and dined on the next day in the refectory with the friars and heard them recite the Canonical Hours in choir. I made the acquaintance accidentally of one of the Canons of the Collegiate Church at Varazze, who, besides showing me his church, accompanied me in a walk through the town and its neighbourhood, pointing out the things most worthy of attention, which, however, were but few. On my mentioning that I had lately been a visitor at San Barnaba, he informed me that he had passed eleven months as a novice in that very convent, but that being unable, physically, to bear "il rigore dell' ordine," he was compelled to leave, and had since become a secular priest. The Canon was polite enough, when I left Varazze, to accompany me a little way out of the town, until, hearing the bell of the Collegiate Church begin to toll in the distance for service, he took leave and returned to take part in the Office. It may serve as an illustration of the timidity entertained in Italy on the score of robbers, and of the absence of the habit of travelling which helps to foster this timidity, that my friend the Canon expressed surprise at my travelling alone on foot, and asked if I did not feel afraid. "Of whom, or what?" was my answer. His reply, "But may you not be killed (ammazzato) by robbers?" amused me from its going, *more Italico*, so straight to the point. An Englishman would, at the most, have hinted the possibility of robbery, while the Italian, without mincing matters, rushed at once to the worst.

However, nothing daunted, I proceeded on my three hours' walk to Savona, carrying in one hand the needful *impedimenta*, and in the other an umbrella to shield my head from the scorching rays of the sun. As far as Celle, where I rested half an hour in the one little *locanda* the place possesses, the road lay along the seashore, and very lovely it was. Afterwards it ran more inland, passing the prettily situated village of Albizzola, until, on approaching Savona, the road returns to the seaboard, which it skirts very finely, winding sharp round the overhanging rocks on the land side. Leaving the highway before entering Savona, I proceeded by a narrow path towards the Capuchin convent near that town, which was to be my destination for the night. I missed my path, and got high up on the hills unable to ascertain in which direction to proceed. Finally, however,

I succeeded in obtaining a little boy as a guide who, although shoeless, conducted me almost at a running pace up and down a succession of stony paths, until just before nightfall we came within view of the convent.

This monastery, like most of its Order, stands on an eminence behind the town. It is unusually large and handsome for a Capuchin convent, and has a pretty church and choir; two cloisters, each forming a quadrangle; a delightful copse or "Bosco;" and an extensive garden. The refectory of this convent consists of a spacious antique-looking chamber or hall, oblong in form, with vaulted roof; and when dimly lighted at the evening meal by two or three oil-lamps made of tin, and suspended at intervals from the ceiling—the friars in their monastic habit and ample beards sitting at the polished oak tables, taking their frugal repast in almost unbroken silence, the quaint figures in the more distant parts of the hall being scarcely discernible in the glimmering light—it felt like a scene reproduced from the middle ages rather than a phase of the actual life of the present day.

In place of the usual little conventual cell, I had assigned to me a room of moderate size with its door opening into one of the cloisters, and two windows commanding a fine view over the seaport town of Savona and the Mediterranean beyond it. This was an apartment reserved for strangers, and it was the only time I had slept on the ground floor of a convent, the sleeping apartments being nearly always on the first (or sometimes on the second) floor, overlooking either the cloister or the open country, according as they happen to be on one side or the other of the corridor that usually extends round the cloister.

The convent bell tolled with the usual frequency, now summoning the community to prayer—now to the refectory—or now, perhaps, announcing the hour of the Ave Maria. It was a sound to which by this time I had become thoroughly accustomed, and yet it seemed always new and suggestive of thought, reminding one by its clockwork regularity, as well as by a certain poetical association that has become attached to the idea of a "convent bell," of the strange ascetic system, the daily routine of which it served to mark.

On the next morning, while still staying at the Savona convent, I took a walk of about two hours through a narrow and beautiful valley to a "Santuario," or Shrine of the Madonna, called Nostra Signora di Misericordia, which dates from three centuries ago, and is of considerable celebrity in this part of Italy. For several miles along the road before arriving at the Santuario, is a series of small chapels dedicated to the Virgin, each of them having a dome, and altogether more pretentious in appearance than such road-side chapels generally are. Halfway between Savona and the Santuario is a niche with an image of the Madonna, bearing the following inscription:—

> "Sistite fratres passus
> Et orate aliquantulùm,
> Hic est medium iter
> Ad Deiparæ templum.
> † 1657. Die 21 A.R.S." (Aprilis).

In passing through a village called San Sebastiano at a short distance from the shrine, I heard music proceeding from a large oratory or chapel adjoining the parish church. On entering, I found it full of people, the seats being arranged sideways like stalls in choirs, those on one side occupied by women, and on the other by men. The congregation were all singing to the accompaniment of an organ, the prayers being recited not by a priest but by a layman in ordinary dress. I was told they were chaunting an Office of the Madonna, and I believe it was one of those instances so common in Italy, of confraternities reciting services of this kind in churches or chapels without the intervention of any clergyman. Just beyond this village is the Santuario itself, being a handsome church richly painted and gilded, and beautifully situated in a sheltered spot surrounded by mountains. Around the church have sprung up several buildings, including a large *ospicio* for the accommodation of pilgrims, and a few cafés

The "Miraculous Image" of Our Lady, to honour which so many resort hither, is placed over the altar of a gorgeously decorated chapel or crypt beneath the church. The steps leading to this chapel descend, as usual in such cases, from the nave. Glasses of water from a spring passing under the feet of the image, were handed to any body who chose to kneel at the altar rails, to be drunk, it is to be presumed, out of devotion to her whom the image represents. Service was going on, at which a number of people were present. I was struck by the very clean and neat appearance of a large school of girls (apparently a charity school) who entered the church walking two and two, dressed in blue frocks and white veils, and preceded by a cross. I was surprised also at finding so many persons in the church assisting at the numerous masses, for there is no town here, and it has been mentioned above how full was the *oratoire* at the neighbouring village of San Sebastiano. I had a scorching walk back to Savona, although it was only the month of April, and I was shaded by an umbrella. I was not sorry to rejoin my monastic hosts at the convent, whom I found already assembled in the refectory at their midday meal.

In the afternoon of the same day I took a walk in company with Padre C— to see the town of Savona, which is an episcopal see, the capital of a province, and a seaport of some size on the road between Nice and Genoa. It has a rather handsome quay skirting the port, and a large and elegant new theatre that does credit to the taste and public spirit of a small provincial town. While the exterior of the cathedral is unfinished and positively frightful in appearance, the interior, which is both spacious and profusely decorated with painting and gilding, is really beautiful. It contains several pictures of note, among them being one of Christ expelling the money-changers from the Temple. The choir is particularly worthy of attention, on account of the curious mosaics in wood with which the stalls are adorned. These consist of representations of various subjects worked in mosaic, woods of different kinds and shades of colour being employed, producing a very striking effect. According to the sacristan of the cathedral, this is reckoned the second church in Italy for mosaics of this description, but I cannot vouch for the correctness of his statement, having seen many fine instances of this kind of workmanship. Savona contains several other churches, some of which I saw, but none appeared to call for particular notice.

Leaving Savona on the next morning (not, however, without an invitation to stop at the convent on my return), I walked to Quiliano, a village nearly two hours distant, the first half of the way lying along the road towards Nice, from which it then diverges and passes through a valley extending from the sea, inland, in a northerly direction. Not far beyond Savona I came to a point in the road where a small stream crosses it, with an old-fashioned bridge for foot passengers on one side. This bridge contained a Latin inscription, which I regret not having copied, to the effect that it was built in the sixteenth century at the public expense, by the care of certain persons named, to whom it gave the title of "equites." At the upper end of the valley above mentioned, is the village of Quiliano, upon a hill immediately overhanging which is perched the pretty convent of Santa Maria degli Angeli.

I had been invited to spend a day or two here by one of the fraternity, Padre L—, who happened to be stopping at Campi whilst I was there. And very glad I was that I had accepted the invitation, for the impression I carried away with me of this convent, and of my stay there, was a most pleasing one. With a brilliant sun and a cloudless sky, grand and beautiful views of mountains on every side, and in the extreme distance southwards the azure blue sea—together with the picturesque, mediæval associations of conventual life, heightened by the solitude of the situation, and the breathless silence that reigned around, broken only by the melodious song of birds, or the deep solemn note of the convent bell—it will not appear surprising that I should retain agreeable reminiscences of my brief sojourn in this peaceful retreat from the tumult and busy interests of the world.

Secluded, however, as this convent is, the

news of the world, at least, if not its spirit, contrived to penetrate even there, for I remember that at my first meal in the refectory, the "Vicario" or Vice-Principal, thinking doubtless to please his guest by tidings of his native country, informed me of the then recent birth of the Princess Beatrice, of which I had not heard before. This struck me as an odd piece of "latest intelligence" to learn within a few days of the occurrence, at a retired rural convent on a mountain top of the Riviera range. The convent of Santa Maria degli Angeli is built on a small scale compared with most Italian monasteries, and the community within its walls was proportionately small, numbering only about half a dozen friars. The Guardian was temporarily absent, having gone to a distance to preach the Lent, from which he had not returned.

On the last morning of my visit, happening to wake very early, and feeling no inclination to sleep, I rose from my bed and leant out of one of the two windows of my cell (for one of the larger cells reserved for "forestieri" or strangers, had been allotted to me), opening into the pretty four-sided cloister. At that delightful hour of a fine spring morning, when all nature seemed in repose, and day was beginning to dawn, I gazed down into the covered passages of the ancient cloister, and thought on the centuries during which they had been trodden by a long succession of men devoted to a religious life, until I could almost have fancied I might behold the *manes* of some of the old monks pacing to and fro in their cloistered walk ! Just then my ears were charmed by the sweet melody of a nightingale, which sent forth its full, clear note in a most exquisite strain. Long did I listen at the open casement to the little creature. I could not see it, but from the loudness of its song, it seemed to be perched somewhere upon the convent itself.

The friars were most unwilling to let me take leave of them after a three days' visit. "Vuole lasciarci ?" said the Vicario in a deprecatory tone ; and before I left he came to my cell and gave me a hearty kiss on each cheek, at the same time warmly inviting me to return another time. From this pretty convent I returned on foot to to the convent at Savona, where I passed the night.

Early next morning I went by diligence back to Voltri, and thence by railway to Genoa. As the diligence entered Voltri, a procession of the Host passed us, preceded by a considerable number of young girls in white dresses and veils, followed by a large number of boys also in holyday dress. These had, I believe, made their first communion that morning. The driver of the diligence stopped his vehicle, and knelt on the ground, while the passengers took off their hats in token of respect to the sacrament. On leaving the diligence I repaired to the church, whither the procession had already arrived. It was crowded with people, many of whom, unable to find room within, were kneeling in the open street.

CHAPTER XIV.

The Certosa of Pavia.

I LEFT the City of Palaces in the first week of May, with the intention of visiting some of the principal towns of Lombardy. Pavia was to be my first destination, partly for its own sake, and partly because I was desirous of seeing the celebrated Certosa, a few miles distant from that city.

At Alessandria the railway train, leaving the main line to Turin, diverges to the north, towards Arona. I quitted the railway at Mortara, and took the diligence for Pavia. Mortara is the capital of a province, and contains 4000 inhabitants. It is conspicuous in contemporary history for having been the scene of a contest between part of the Austrian army and the Piedmontese in 1849, and also for having been temporarily occupied by the Austrians in the campaign of ten years later. The Church of Santa Croce, nearly opposite the hotel, contains an old and curious painting on wood of the Adoration of the Three Kings, and the impress in marble of a foot, said by tradition to be that of the Saviour, over which is inscribed, "Adorabunt vestigia pedum tuorum."

The journey from Mortara to Pavia occupied about four hours, the country being throughout quite level, and most uninteresting. We passed several small towns, of which Garlasco appeared the largest and most important. At one point in the road was a cemetery, in passing which the driver of the diligence took off his hat, holding it for a few moments in his hand during which he seemed to be offering up a silent prayer. He afterwards said it is usual in passing a cemetery to repeat a prayer or psalm, such as the Paternoster or De Profundis, for the souls in purgatory. At what was then the last village on the Sardinian side were a number of cafés to which I was told "i signori" walked over from Pavia to read the journals that were prohibited under the paternal government of Austria, and where they could converse more freely than at home. On my expressing surprise that the Austrians permitted this to be done, my informant replied that the "signori" in question being regularly provided with passports, it would be difficult to hinder them. Soon after leaving this village, we came to the frontier, where, I being the only passenger excepting three or four country people without luggage, my things came in for a full share of overhauling. But it was my books to which the officials directed their main attention. Every book, English, French, Latin &c., was separately examined. All were pronounced to be unexceptionable until the last, a volume of Essays on Political Economy, was opened. The *douanier* called a superior officer and inquired whether it was admissible, but the latter, after due examination, apparently feeling the responsibility of deciding so knotty a point, sent for a third official of still higher grade. This personage made his appearance in a few minutes, and having read over the title page (whether understanding its meaning or not, I cannot say) declared it might pass. Probably it was the word "political" which had given rise to all this hesitation. I must, nevertheless, remark that in few continental countries was so little trouble given to travellers in regard to passports, and, generally, in respect of examination of luggage also, as in Lombardy at the period of my visit. I travelled through the Lombardo-Venetian provinces, stopping at nearly all the principal towns, and finally left the

Austrian territories, without having my passport viséd or asked for again after first entering the country. Neither was there any examination of passengers' effects at Milan or the other large towns. I heard, however, that this relaxation of restrictions in the case of Austrian Italy had been but recently introduced.

Passing over the river Ticino by a handsome stone bridge, covered in with a wooden roof, you find yourself at once in the main street of Pavia, which commences where the bridge ends. There is a picturesqueness about the general aspect of Pavia that constitutes it, to my mind, quite a type of an Italian provincial town. The approach by the covered bridge over the river is imposing, and more so still is the exit towards the Certosa by a fine double avenue of horse-chestnuts. The chief object of interest within the town itself, is the extensive and handsome series of buildings forming the University, which once enjoyed a European reputation as a seat of learning. And even now it is far from being deserted, numbering as it does nearly one thousand students. The principal churches are the Cathedral and the Italian Gothic church of the Carmine. Many of the streets are lined with covered walks, or arcades, which form a conspicuous feature in most of the Lombard cities. Little is known of Pavia in ancient times except its classical name of *Ticinum*, from the river on whose banks it stands. At a later period this was changed to Papia, which became softened into Pavia, the accent in Italian being on the penultimate.

But the great attraction to the visitor to Pavia is the magnificent Certosa, or Carthusian Priory of La Beata Vergine delle Grazie, five miles distant from the town. This monastery is considered by some to be the most splendid convent in the world. The earlier part of the road to it is lined by an avenue of immense horse-chestnut trees, previously adverted to, whose overhanging branches and abundant foliage form a welcome shade from an Italian sun, as well as a highly picturesque object to the view, as the traveller leaves or approaches Pavia. After proceeding for several miles along the highway, you diverge to the right by a lane leading up to the Certosa, which stands alone in an extensive plain, away from any town or village. As you come in view of this celebrated monastery, there is little in its exterior to tell of the treasury of art that it encloses. For, built in a warlike age, it bears at first sight the appearance of a baronial castle rather than the abode of peaceful monks, being surrounded by a wall and moat, with a massive arched gateway. Passing under the portal, (which is adorned with frescoes, chiefly by Luini) you enter a spacious courtyard, with the beautiful front of one of the finest churches in Italy before you.

The Certosa of Pavia, after an existence of nearly 400 years, was included in the suppression of the religious houses in the Austrian dominions by the Emperor Joseph II. towards the end of the last century. Accordingly, travellers in the earlier part of the present century speak of it as suppressed, and therefore shorn of much of its monastic associations. But of late years it has again become a monastery of living monks. Its cells and wonderful cloisters, and splendid refectory, and stately church, are once more tenanted by Carthusians in their white habit and cowl. The matin bell again resounds over the surrounding plains at the solemn hour of midnight; and the beautiful bronze gates that guard the "clausura" or monastic enclosure, are, as in former times, impassable to the "devotus fœmineus sexus," unless provided with a special brief from the Pope.* The Certosa

* This, as before noticed, is the general rule in mo-

was restored not only to monastic purposes, but to its original Order, in the year 1835, and at the period of my visit had the appearance of being in a highly flourishing state. The community consisted at that time of a Prior and twenty-seven other monks.

The priory church is a most grand specimen, internally, of the best style of Italian Gothic, and is equal in dimensions and in beauty to a fine cathedral. The florid Lombard front of this church is superb, and the entire edifice is

nasteries of men; and I was informed by one of the monks of the Certosa of Pavia, that such is the case in that monastery in particular. I knew two Catholic ladies who, in company with a priest, made an excursion from Milan to this Certosa, one of them being provided with a Papal brief, and the other hoping, as her companion, and supported too by the authority of her clerical friend, to be admitted. The lady named in the brief, and the priest, were shewn over the convent, but the second lady had to content herself with seeing only the church. The reader will be amused to hear that in the brief referred to, it is directed that the lady shall be conducted through the monastery by three of the elder monks—" senioribus ;" that her visit is to be made between sunrise and sunset; and that a bell is to be rung before her as she proceeds, in order, doubtless, to warn the fraternity to flee from the danger to which they might be exposed from so unaccustomed a visitor!

worthy to be classed among the finest churches of which Italy can boast. The façade is of marble, and is divided by four pilasters and two turrets into five spaces, which are filled by a mass of beautiful sculpture. Six statues adorn each of the pilasters and turrets, and the highly decorated portico in the centre of the front is enriched by master-pieces of sculpture. Over the portico is a triforium of the Tuscan order, reaching across the whole façade, and above this is a dedication to the Virgin, who is described as " mother, daughter, bride of God." The interior of this church forms so valuable a museum of paintings, sculpture, mosaics, bas-reliefs, marbles, carving in wood, and altars inlaid with precious stones, that to describe them in detail would fill a volume. The nave is separated from the transepts and choir, and from the side chapels, by a partition consisting of lofty bronze gates of very elegant design. This marks the *clausura*. The workmanship of these gates is so elaborate as to constitute them a beautiful work of art

It would be difficult to give an idea of the splendour of the High Altar and Choir, profusely decorated with exquisite stone carving and with admirable mosaics in wood, of which latter the whole of the stalls consist; while the magnificence of the larger of the two Sacristies, of the Lavatory of the monks, of the principal Cloister* and the Refectory literally defies description. The refectory is so splendid in regard both to its size and decorations, that it is probably surpassed by few halls in Europe. It is used only on Sundays and holydays, for on other days each monk takes his meals privately in his own apartment, his food being handed to him from the cloister through a small aperture in the wall, which is closed by a wooden shutter when not in use. Every Carthusian in holy orders has a separate apartment, comprising three or four chambers, including an oratory, which collectively are called his "casa" or house. These "case" are placed contiguous to one another, round the cloister.

The whole monastery is, in a word, *sui generis*. Its magnificent splendour, especially that of the vast and lovely cloister, added to the prevalence of the round arch, recalled to my mind at the time the descriptions of the Alhambra. The Carthusian Order, to which it

* This immense and beautiful cloister is 412 feet long, and 334 wide. The second cloister is adorned by numerous bas-reliefs in terra-cotta of rare merit.

belongs, was founded by St. Bruno in the eleventh century. It is among the strictest of the religious Orders. The monks rise to matins at midnight; and both then and throughout the day they spend an unusual length of time in prayer. Their method of singing the Canonical Hours is celebrated for its extreme slowness, thus admitting of the words being fully meditated upon. Silence is enjoined as an essential virtue, and is much exercised among them, although not so absolutely, I believe, as it is by the Trappists. The Carthusians abstain altogether from meat, and otherwise fast very rigorously. They are allowed, once a week, to walk out in community for exercise, retired places being selected for the purpose. This Order enjoys the reputation of having preserved the original severity of its Rule undiminished after the lapse of eight centuries; and, according to Roman Catholic historians, it has the honour of being one of the few monastic Orders that have never either received, or required, a reform. Another characteristic of the Carthusians is that, while their life is exceedingly rigid, their monasteries rank amongst the finest in the world in regard to architecture and decorations, as well as in extent.*

* At the Reformation this austere Order numbered

The Certosa of Pavia is interesting not only for its artistic beauty, and for the monastic traditions of the celebrated Order to which it belongs, but also for the historical reminiscences connected with it. Founded by Galeazzo Visconti, first duke of Milan, in 1396, this stately fabric, with its gorgeous decorations, required a century to finish it. Not many years had elapsed from the time of its completion, when its immediate neighbourhood became the scene of a battle in which Francis I. of France was defeated by the Imperialists, and he himself made prisoner. He was conducted, according to a tradition, to this Certosa, having, as he said, "lost everything save honour." It is related that as he entered the priory church after this reverse of fortune, the monks, who were chaunting a psalm, were joined in their chaunt by the French king when they came to the words, " Bonum mihi quia humiliasti me, ut discam justificationes tuas."

nine houses in England, of which the one in London, the Charterhouse, still retains its name. Another was at Sheen in Surrey. Nine is the number that the Order had in Italy at the period of my visit. In the last century, the total number of Carthusian monasteries in the world was 172.—See the Life of St. Bruno, in Alban Butler's " Lives of the Saints."

I left Pavia on the afternoon of the 8th of May, and in three hours and a half entered the capital of Lombardy. The road by which I travelled passed over a fertile but otherwise uninteresting plain, a considerable part of which, in common with much of the Milanese, is devoted to the cultivation of rice, indicated by the extensive sheets of water under which the rice fields lay nearly concealed from view.

CHAPTER XV.

The Cathedral of Milan, and sundry Monasteries in Northern Italy.

It is not my intention to fill these pages with a description of Milan, or the other places that I visited during a journey from that city through Lombardy to Venice, and thence southwards to Naples by Florence and Rome. This journey, it is true, was fraught with the highest interest. Architecture, painting, sculpture, classical associations, and lovely scenery, all combined to render it interesting and delightful in no ordinary degree; but I am unwilling to go over ground that has been so often trodden by other travellers. My conventual experiences, however, form, I believe, a new path amid the highways and byewnys of Italian travelling, and I shall continue to confine myself almost exclusively to these, touching only very lightly on matters which, although possibly of more general and varied interest, are better known to the reading public. I cannot, however, forbear saying a few words on the Cathedral of Milan, which I consider to be the grandest architectural effort of human genius that I have seen in Italy or out of it. In the present chapter I purpose giving a short account of this Queen of Gothic churches, and also of several large and interesting monasteries that I visited in the course of my journey.

The Cathedral of Milan stands in the centre of the city, and in the principal piazza, of which it forms one side. Its architecture is Gothic, and although not of the perfectly pure form of that style to which we are accustomed in the stately Gothic cathedrals of England, France and Belgium, it far more nearly approaches to the best Gothic type than most Italian churches to which that term is applied. Built of white marble—prodigious in length, breadth, and height—Gothic in character—a mass of florid decorations, including no less than 7000 statuettes placed in elegant niches—this church is one of the most magnificent that has ever been erected. Second in dimensions only to the Vatican, it is equal in length to the Cathedral of Florence and St. Paul's, while in breadth it exceeds both. Its lavish profusion of gracefully formed Gothic turrets and pinnacles is another of the peculiarities of the Cathedral of Milan. It has been pronounced by a competent judge to excel in point of fretwork, carving and statues, all churches in the world.* I know nothing with which to compare the effect produced by a view of this splendid edifice from the eastern end. So profuse and so delicately executed is the marble-wrought fretwork by which the whole of the exterior is adorned—resembling in its exquisitely florid workmanship a mass of lace carved in marble—that an appearance of airy lightness and fragile elegance is imparted to it which almost suggests the idea of its being liable to be blown away from lack of stability, until you remember that the vast and beautiful fabric before you is hewn out of marble.

A sight equally beautiful, but quite different in character, meets the eye on entering the cathedral. Here, instead of lightness and elegance, is sombre gloom—the dim light and impressive gloom so well known to, and appreciated by, the admirers of Northern Gothic, and for the loss of which all the grandeur and beauty of St. Peter's itself could not compensate. This master-piece of architecture combines in its interior the vastness of St. Peter's, the subdued Gothic light and imposing solemnity of Rouen,

* Eustace's 'Classical Tour.'

and the profusion of painted glass of St. Denis. Its hundred and sixty lofty columns (more than ninety feet in height and eight in diameter) its broad double aisles, its brilliant coating of polished marble, and its handsome pavement made of different coloured marbles arranged in various patterns, are all calculated to excite the admiration of the spectator. The peculiar and ungothic form of the capitals of the columns, however, and the painted tracery of the roof, both appeared to me to detract somewhat from the Gothic effect of the whole.

In a crypt, beneath the nave, is the sumptuous shrine of St. Charles Borromeo, whose body is kept there. The sacristy of the cathedral contains a "tesoro," or treasure of great value, consisting of two massive silver statues of the patrons of Milan, St. Ambrose and St. Charles Borromeo, in their episcopal vestments, and a number of immense silver candlesticks, several valuable chalices and remonstrances, and other articles of church furniture. The mitres, vestments and croziers on the above named statues of the two archbishops are richly ornamented with jewels, and the estimated value of each of the statues is enormous—I forget how many hundred thousand crowns.

It is only from the roof of the cathedral that any just conception can be formed of the mass of florid fretwork, carving and sculpture by which the entire building is covered. Many of the statues on the inner sides of the turrets are not visible except from the roof itself, and among these is one by Canova. If the reader will endeavour to realize to himself the effect produced by *seven thousand* marble statues, each placed in a highly florid Gothic niche, every space between them being overlaid with carving and fretwork, he may possibly have some idea of the appearance of this singular and magnificent church. The figures are in fact statues, not statuettes, though they look like the latter to the naked eye when seen from below. The view from the roof of the cathedral over the surrounding country, with the Alps rising majestically in the background, is very beautiful.

The liturgy of the Church of Milan differs in some respects from that used by the Roman Church generally, the Milanese having always preserved the liturgy which, from being reformed by St. Ambrose, has received the appellation of "Ambrosian." I procured in the sacristy of the cathedral an Ambrosian Missal

and Breviary, and on comparing them with
the Roman, found that they differed in several
small matters of detail, but that the services
were essentially the same. I heard high mass
celebrated in the cathedral according to the
Ambrosian rite. I was struck on this and on
several other occasions when I visited the
cathedral (and other churches of Milan also)
with the decided preponderance of the male sex
among the congregation—a very unusual circumstance either in Catholic or Protestant
countries. The chapter of the metropolitan
church of Milan is on a scale commensurate
with the splendour of the edifice itself, consisting of twenty-eight Mitred Canons, who
officiate with episcopal ceremony, besides
twenty simple or unmitred Canons.

For the reasons already given, I do not stop
to describe my journey from Milan to Brescia
and the Lake of Garda, or thence by Verona
and Vicenza to Padua; but proceed at once to
give some account of my visit to the great
conventual church and convent of St. Antony
of Padua, which is first among the many
objects of interest by which Padua is enriched.
This pleasant and beautiful town may be described as a City of Domes and Arcades; the

eight mosque-like domes of the Church of St. Antony and those of Sta. Giustina, the Duomo, the Carmine, and other churches, bearing out the former epithet, while the numerous colonnaded streets illustrate the latter.

The Church of St. Antony of Padua is a stately edifice, and the chapel containing the saint's body is a splendid specimen of a shrine. The devotion at Padua to St. Antony seems extraordinarily great, a fact, by the way, that made an impression on Addison, a century and a half ago. On each of the principal streets leading to the church (although it is not the cathedral) are inscribed the words, "Al Santo," with a hand pointing in that direction. Addison describes how, at the period of his visit to Italy, the people thronged around this shrine, and in their devotional zeal pressed their lips against the marble of which it is formed. The very same scene presented itself to the view at the time of my visit in 1857; for on each of the several occasions that I entered this church, numerous persons were crowding up to the back of the altar where St. Antony of Padua's body rests, desirous of impressing a kiss upon the monument containing the saint's ashes.

St. Antony of Padua flourished in the early part of the thirteenth century. He is usually represented in paintings with the infant Jesus in his arms. He was born at Lisbon, and was among the first disciples of St. Francis of Assisi. He is especially celebrated for his humility, in illustration of which it is related of him, that wishing to enter a monastery, and happening to apply for admittance to several, where it seems learning and capacity for preaching were more in request than ability for manual labour, he was constantly refused admittance, because he professed himself fit only for such menial offices as washing the floors, and cooking. Finally, however, his attainments accidentally became known, and he was soon regarded as one of the lights of the newly founded Franciscan Order. He taught for a short time in the schools of Padua, but died at an early age, in the year after his arrival there. The Portuguese also pay great honour to St. Antony as their countryman.

The Church of St. Antony of Padua belongs to Franciscan Friars of the Order of Conventuals, called in Italy "Conventuali," of whom there were here upwards of fifty at the time of my visit. They wear a black habit, with a thin white cord round the waist instead of the thick cord worn by other Franciscans. The Conventuals are no longer mendicants, being the only branch of the Franciscan Order that professedly receives endowments. Their Superior is styled " Guardiano" or " Guardian," in common with the Superiors of all Franciscan houses of every branch; for the humble St. Francis thought the titles of Abbot and Prior savoured too much of worldly pomp and dignity to allow his disciples to make use of them. The monastery is extensive and contains three distinct cloisters, each of them forming a complete quadrangle. These are entered from the church, at the side of which they are successively placed; and one, if not two, of them being outside the monastic enclosure, may be visited by ladies. An iron gate, with the inscription "Clausura," marks the point where the enclosure begins. The dormitories of this convent are remarkable for their great breadth, giving them rather the appearance of spacious halls than of ordinary corridors. The general effect of the fine church of St. Antony of Padua, with its immense size and oriental domes, is seen to full advantage from the large open piazza in which it stands.

I should regret that the scope of this volume does not admit of my attempting any description of beautiful Venice, had not the Queen of the Adriatic been so often described by poets and painters, as well as by travellers, as to render its beauties well known to almost every reader. Who is not familiar with the lovely palaces of Venice, their marble walls washed by the charming canals by which the city is intersected in every direction? Or with the venerable Palace of the Doges, the noble Basilica of St. Mark, and the splendid square of the same name? The famous Rialto, and the no less famous gondolas, and the celebrated Galleries of Paintings at Venice, also form too favourite a theme with Italian travellers, to render it necessary or desirable to enlarge on them here.

From Venice I travelled by Padua and Ferrara to Bologna. Bologna, yet more than Padua, may be called a City of Arcades, nearly all the streets being covered in by arched galleries. The two Leaning Towers, the Church of San Petronio, the University, and, above all, the fine Gallery of Paintings, are the chief objects of interest at Bologna; but I shall confine my remarks to the Dominican Church and Convent there, both of which merit particular notice. The church contains a beautiful marble altar-tomb of St. Dominic, with exquisitely sculptured figures, one of which is attributed to Michael Angelo. The tomb forms the altar of a large side-chapel, and is a light, elegant and finely-executed mass of statuettes, bas-reliefs, and other sculpture, the whole constituting a splendid specimen of a sepulchral monument. It struck me as a marked and pleasing contrast to the heavy, sombre character of most modern sepulchral architecture. The celebrated Tombs of the Scaligeri* at Verona, produced a similar impression on my mind, their light, graceful and picturesque effect being quite delightful when compared with many of the heavy, meaningless

---

* In general character the Tombs of the Scaligeri bear a resemblance to the light fretwork of some of the tombs in Winchester cathedral. The effect of those at Verona is increased by the entire tomb standing, not upon the ground, but on several slender columns, perhaps eight or ten feet in height, thus admitting of a passage under them, and presenting altogether a very graceful appearance, enhanced, too, by their being *sub Dio* in the small cemetery of a little church in the middle of the town.

monuments in St. Paul's; or with some of the sepulchres of the greatest men to whom Italy has given birth contained in Santa Croce at Florence; or with some of the tombs of the Popes even in St. Peter's. In each of these instances, an essentially depressing subject— death—is rendered still more so by the heavy, lugubrious method of treating it. A ponderous mass of stone or marble for a base, with several semi-naked allegorical figures of the Virtues at top, seems to be the modern idea in Italy, as well as in our own less artistic land, of what sepulchral monuments should consist.

The only part of this allegorical style of tombs worth looking at, is usually the statue of the "illustrious dead" himself, who of course stands, or sits enthroned, in the midst of the "Virtues" aforesaid. It seems to me, that the effort in such works should be to divert the mind from the gloomy side of a painful subject by exhibiting something beautiful and gracefully light in character; or, at least, that they should be so grand and imposing in form and size as to excite the soul to corresponding sentiments, and thus, in another way, to turn aside the thoughts from the literal fact of death. Ancient feeling adopted the latter—the grand style—mediæval art the former, that is the light and graceful character. The pyramids, and the two mausoleums of Adrian and of Cecilia Metella at Rome, are instances of the one; the beautiful sepulchral monuments in Winchester cathedral, the elegant tomb of St. Dominic at Bologna, and the tombs of the Scaligeri, are examples of the other. Each of these half dozen ancient and middle-age tombs is regarded as a fine work of art in itself; but who would care to visit most of the monuments in St. Paul's, or many even of those in Santa Croce, if divested of the associations connected with the names to whose honour they were erected? Would any person, five hundred years hence, care to see Nelson's monument, or Canova's miniature pyramid, as artistic productions independent of the memory of the eminent admiral or sculptor? But the interest of the great pyramid, on the contrary, does not depend merely on the memory of King Cheops, nor that of the castle of St. Angelo on the Emperor Adrian, nor of the Verona tombs on our sympathy with the Scaligeri. In the one set of examples, the monument, either by its grandeur or its intrinsic beauty, preserves the memory of the dead: in the other, the memory of the dead alone imparts interest to the monument.

The roof of the Chapel of St. Dominic is adorned with a splendid fresco by Guido, considered to be one of his finest fresco paintings. On the opposite side of the church is Guido's own monument, he having been buried here in the same tomb with Elizabeth Sirani, a painter of great reputation, who is said to have died of poison at the age of twenty-six, administered by some fellow artists from jealousy of her rising talents. I was conducted over the adjoining convent by a very intelligent Friar. This convent was founded by St. Dominic in the year 1217, and from that time up to the French Revolution, at least, it continued to be one of the most flourishing monasteries in the world. It is of considerable size, although part of it was then occupied by Austrian soldiers. The chief object of interest that I saw there, was an extensive library, forming an elegant suite of rooms, and enriched by a numerous collection of books. The religious community at the period of my visit consisted of about thirty friars.

I accomplished the journey from Bologna to Florence over the Appenines, by Pistoia, in about sixteen hours. The ascent of the Appenines was exceedingly beautiful, although less grand than the Alpine passes. When, after a toiling ascent, you reach the summit of the Appenine range, and commence the descent, the effect is very striking; for, on emerging from the winding defiles of the mountains, you suddenly see stretched out before you the extensive and luxuriantly fertile plain, in the foreground of which lies Pistoia, at the base of the Appenines you are rapidly descending, while in the extreme distance rises the imposing outline of Firenze la Bella.

This was not my first visit to Florence, but I was more than ever pleased with it. It ranks, in my estimation, among the most beautiful cities of Italy. It is delightfully situated at the foot of the Appenines, by which it is partly encircled, the mountains extending on one side up to the town itself. The principal portion of the city lies between the base of the Appenines and the Arno, although a considerable part is on the opposite bank of the river, which thus divides Florence into two unequal halves, connected by four handsome bridges. But the scenery amid which Florence is situated, lovely as that is, is only an accessory to its other beauties, so beautiful is the town itself, and the numerous picturesque and artistic objects it contains. Among these are the thoroughly mediæval Piazza del Granduca, with the stately Palazzo

Vecchio, a chef-d'œuvre of architecture, on one side of it, and on another the elegant Loggia dei Lanzi, a beautiful open gallery supported on arches and embellished by several fine pieces of sculpture in stone and bronze. Among the other beautiful points of view in Florence are the Piazzas of the Duomo, of Santa Maria Novella, and of La Trinità, and the Cascine, or public garden, with its groves of lofty forest trees, bordered on one side by the Arno, and on the other by the Appenines. The palaces of Florence are of a peculiar style of architecture, the Tuscan, which is of a very sombre character, although particularly beautiful. The churches also partake of the same heavy, solemn style as the Florentine palaces. Among the principal churches are the cathedral, Santa Croce, Santo Spirito, and Santa Maria Novella, all of them exceedingly fine. But as I do not propose to describe these, or the splendid collections of sculpture and painting in the Uffizi or Pitti Palaces, I will proceed at once to the subject I have selected for special notice at Florence, viz., the Convent of San Marco, which is full of interest, historical and artistic, as well as monastic.[*]

[*] San Marco is described in this chapter for the sake of convenience, although it cannot strictly be included under the head of monasteries of Northern Italy.

The convent of San Marco, besides the architectural and artistic interest attaching to it, possesses an historical celebrity from its connection with Savonarola, who was a Dominican friar, and Prior of San Marco. The reader will remember how by his extraordinary preaching and exemplary life, Savonarola gained such an ascendency over his fellow-citizens, that although unpossessed of any official authority, he had nearly the whole city under his control. Savonarola was essentially a monk in character and feeling, as well as in name. A man of virtuous life and enthusiastic temperament, he was deeply scandalized at the gross irregularities that prevailed among both laity and clergy. To reform the latter, he not only thundered from the pulpit against the morals of ecclesiastics in general, but he singled out great dignitaries, and even the Pope himself by name for severe denunciation; while, in regard to the laity, he sought to reform them by using the great influence he possessed over the Florentines to induce the whole population to adopt almost a monastic rigidity of discipline, in which he is said to have succeeded to a considerable extent by the unaided efforts of his own strong will and saintly life.

However, after a time a change came over popular feeling, and the Prior of St. Mark's having made great enemies among those in authority, several circumstances concurred to cause him to be sentenced to death. Savonarola was burnt at the stake, or, according to some, first hanged, and then burnt, in the Piazza del Granduca, near the Loggia dei Lanzi, on the 23rd of May, 1498. His portrait may be seen in the convent " Spezieria," or pharmacy.

I went over this monastery, which is reckoned among the finest in Florence. It still belongs to the Dominican Order. The cloisters, of which there are two sets, are beautiful. In these and other parts of the convent are preserved several exquisite masterpieces, in fresco, by Beato Angelico da Fiesole, who was a friar of San Marco, and whose frescoes are among the very finest existing. Of these, two of the best are in the dormitories, near each other, and the third in a cell, believed to have been that of Savonarola. They all represent the Madonna, and in each, the combined expression of sweetness and devotion is charming beyond measure. Beneath one of the frescoes in the dormitories is the inscription, " Virginis intactæ cùm veneris ante figuram, prætereundo cave ne sileatur." Not far from this is another fresco by B. Angelico, and here the guide who conducted me over the convent seemed unable to restrain his enthusiasm. The fresco in question represents the child Jesus with his mother, and after descanting on its beauty, the guide exclaimed with warmth—speaking of the infant Jesus—" Ma non è umano, è proprio divino, è l'unico, veda che grazia e che pietà nella faccia !"*

As I returned through the quiet, shady cloisters, a sight thoroughly monastic struck my eye. Passing along the opposite side of the quadrangle to that in which I stood, were eight young men habited entirely in white, with hoods drawn over their heads, walking two and two at a measured pace, in silence. I stopped to look at them, but in less than a minute they had passed through a doorway leading out of the cloister and disappeared. A bell was tolling, doubtless to summon them to some part of their strict daily routine. In a few months more these novices would probably all have taken the monastic vows—all have bound themselves irrevocably, for better for worse, to the rigid discipline and self-denial of a religious state. The community of San Marco when I visited it, consisted of nearly forty friars, including the novices. The convent church is

* "It (the expression of the face) is not human—it is truly divine—there is nothing like it—see what grace and piety are depicted in the countenance!"

adorned by many excellent fresco and other paintings, as well as by several fine statues and bronzes.

From Florence I travelled, by Sienna, to Rome. I was much pleased with Sienna, the narrow, winding, hilly streets of which, and its vast mediæval-looking Piazza, are most picturesque. The cathedral is a superb specimen of Italian florid Gothic, and is in my opinion one of the finest churches in Italy. I went over the Benedictine Abbey and Church of San Domenico at Sienna. The church is interesting from its great size, and for possessing several beautiful frescoes of very early date. The abbey itself is small, and was indebted for any interest attaching to it, partly to the distinguished Order to which it now belongs, and partly to its having been inhabited by St. Catherine of Sienna, when it was a convent of Dominican nuns, which it continued to be till the French Revolution. At Rome I rested for a few weeks, refreshing my mind amid its glorious memories and unparalleled works of art. Thence I proceeded southwards, by Terracina, to Naples, along a line of road, of which nearly every mile teems with classical associations.

CHAPTER XVI.

Convents at Naples.

NAPLES is the most populous, the gayest, and the most splendidly situated of all the cities of Italy. It stands at the base of a mountain on the shore of a bay nearly thirty miles in diameter, bordered on the right by the promontory of Miseno, and on the left by that of Sorrento, the beautiful Island of Capri, with its craggy peaks, rising in the centre, and forming a charming addition to the general view. To the left, or south side of the city, is Vesuvius, its column of vapoury smoke ever rising to the clouds; and along the sea shore in the same direction extend in close contiguity the towns of Portici, Resina, Torre del Greco and others; while along the northern coast lie the Islands of Nisida, Procida, and Ischia, the lofty rocks of the latter being majestically grand, even as seen from Naples, whence the distance is considerable. It need hardly be added that the beauty of the situation is greatly enhanced by the deep blue of both sky and sea, which seem to vie with one another in the southern richness of their colouring.

The cheerful gaiety of Naples is one of its principal characteristics. With a population of half a million persons, crowded into narrow streets, which are traversed by a large number of carriages, public and private, there is a constant appearance of activity and excitement that reminds you more of London and Paris than of an Italian town. Nor is this busy stirring aspect of the place diminished by the absence, for the most part, of foot-pavements, leading of course to a frequent intermingling of the passengers and the carriages, although, like many other practical inconveniences in Continental life, it has its picturesque side. Indeed, the traveller must ever bear in mind the fact that Italy would cease to be Italy—together with the charming associations connected with the name—if its people and their habits were to be moulded according to the stiff conventionalities, and cold proprieties, and prosaic conveniences of English life.

The most striking parts of the city of Naples, are the Strada Toledo—the principal street—long and narrow, and lined with shops; the Chiaja, or public promenade and drive on the seashore, at the western end of the town; the spacious quay bordering on the busy and well filled port to the south; and the great squares called respectively the Largo di Palazzo, and the Largo del Castello, which, both from their great size and the edifices they contain, are particularly handsome.

I am almost tempted to diverge from the main purpose of this volume, in order to describe the wonderful and unrivalled specimen of an ancient town that Pompeii exhibits, at a distance of thirteen miles south of Naples; and also the magnificent, and in some respects unequalled museum, called the Studii Publici, at Naples itself—to say nothing of the many objects of minor interest with which this city abounds. But recollecting that all these interesting subjects have been often, and for the most part fully described, I am recalled from such a digression to the special subject to which, with few exceptions, I have confined my remarks. It is not, then, from lack of taking interest in other matters connected with beautiful Naples that I proceed at once to give some account of the principal religious houses which I visited there.

Foremost among these was the great Certosa of San Martino, perched on the top of the hill of Sant' Elmo, which overhangs Naples, in immediate proximity to the fort of the same name. The church, which is more frequently visited by travellers than the convent, is celebrated for its architecture, and for the excellence of its paintings, as well as for the value and beauty of its marbles and precious stones. The monastery itself, over which I was conducted by one of the white-habited and black-bearded lay-brothers, is large and very handsome. It contains two cloisters, one of which is built with Carthusian magnificence, in respect both of its immense size and the elegance of its construction. It is supported by sixty-four columns of marble, being sixteen on each side of the spacious quadrangle which the cloister encloses. The "case," or separate sets of three rooms for each monk, extend round the cloister, with a small aperture for receiving food from without, as mentioned in describing the Certosa of Pavia. The number of monks at the time of my visit was thirty-one.

The windows of this monastery, and also its extensive garden, command a beautiful view of the entire Bay of Naples. This was the finest view of the Bay I had yet seen. In front of the spectator, a few miles out to sea, lies the charming Island of Capri, while Vesuvius rises majestically on the left, with the Appenines in the background; and farther southward, along the sea-board, extend Sant' Angelo and other mountains, among which Sorrento may be discerned in the distance. On the right, or northwards, beyond the hill of Posilipo, you see the Island of Ischia, the effect of whose rocky mass rising grandly from the blue sea, as beheld from the elevated position of San Martino, is fine in the extreme. Below you, at the base of the hill on which you are standing, is stretched out the great and populous city of Naples, the hum of human voices, and the rolling of the carriages resounding, even at this height, like an echo of distant thunder. Altogether, the view was splendid, and realized my ideal of the beauties of the Bay of Naples.

Another of the most interesting convents of Naples or its neighbourhood, is that of the Camaldolesi Hermits, situated upon the summit of a wooded mountain on the northern side of Naples, and commanding a magnificent panoramic view, for which it is celebrated. The convent is approached by a steep mule-path, cut through a thick and shady wood, which seems to form an appropriate barrier between the hermits and the outer world.* I was particularly desirous of visiting this monastery, because houses of its austere Order are rare, and I had never before had the opportunity of entering one. At a short distance from the large and antiquated-looking convent gateway, is an inscription on a stone boundary-mark, surmounted by a cross, to the effect that women cannot pass beyond that point under pain of excommunication. The inscription was in Italian, with the addition at the end, of two Latin words, "latæ sententiæ," the meaning of which expression, however, would probably not be very intelligible to most of the "femine," for whose benefit it appeared to be inscribed.

The monastery stands quite alone on this lofty hill, isolated from all human habitations. It realizes the idea of monastic retirement, not only from its isolation, but also from the forest of wood by which it is surrounded. The convent is encompassed by a high wall, which together with a massive stone gateway forming the old feudal-looking entrance, reminds you of a mediæval stronghold. After pulling the bell

* It was at least by such a path that I approached it, although I believe there is a carriage way by a more circuitous road.

several times, and then waiting until leave could be obtained from the Superior for my admittance, I was at length received by one of the Hermits, named Fra Luca, who politely conducted me over the different parts of the monastery, or more properly speaking, *hermitage*; for unlike religious Orders generally—who live in cells contiguous to one another in the same building, and meet together for meals in a common refectory—the Camaldolesi Hermits inhabit separate small houses, each standing quite detached, one of which is appropriated to every monk. The whole are comprised within an enclosure formed by a high wall, and in these houses the monks live entirely, taking their meals in solitude, and using no refectory. Nor is there any cloister, so that the appearance of the monastery is that of a church, and a number of little detached houses arranged in rows, enclosed within a space of ground bounded by an outer wall.

It is from this practice of living alone in their separate houses, and thus more completely secluded from each other than most monastic Orders, that they derive their name of Hermits. In this respect the Carthusians somewhat resemble them; for the Carthusians, as previously explained, use no common refectory except on festas, and each monk has a little suite of several rooms, called his *casa*, or house. But these, in the case of the Carthusians, of Italy at least,* are not detached houses, being merely apartments in the same building, and all opening into the cloister, which in Carthusian monasteries is usually on a scale of extraordinary size and beauty.

Fra Luca, a lay-brother of the Order, informed me that the Camaldolesi Hermits never leave the convent, with the single exception of the Padre Procuratore, or steward, and that they devote a larger part of the day to prayer and religious exercises, than even the religious Orders in general. Besides the Seven Canonical Hours of the Breviary, in the recital of which, according to my informant, they occupy so long a time, as seemed scarcely credible, they recite the "Seven Canonical Hours of the Madonna," and moreover spend an hour and a half in meditation, three quarters of an hour in devotional reading, (if I remember right), besides

* The Chartreuses in France, however, resemble the Camaldolesi Monastery at Naples in point of construction, consisting of a number of detached houses enclosed by a wall.

other exercises in addition. They sing Matins in the middle of the night, and recite the Office in choir in community, which is the only occasion on which they assemble together. I am not aware whether they are prohibited from conversing when they meet in the garden, or from making occasional short visits to one another in their respective houses.

Fra Luca also told me that each padre or priest has three rooms and a chapel in his house, with a small garden adjoining it; but that the lay-brothers have one room only. He likewise informed me that the number of monks at this monastery was twenty-seven, of whom fourteen were priests, and thirteen lay-brothers. The view from the garden over the Bay of Naples is most extensive and very lovely, but I saw it under a great disadvantage, for the sky was overcast by angry-looking clouds that threatened a storm, and of course interfered with the beauty of the view, although they imparted to it a sombre grandeur of their own.

Nowhere, perhaps, is there to be found a more complete type of the monastic and eremitical life than is afforded by this ancient and secluded monastery, with its ascetic inmates.

Whilst descending through the woods by the mule-path towards Naples, my thoughts were naturally led to reflect on the contrast between the rigid and contemplative life passed within the Hermitage I had just left, and the active pleasure-seeking existence of the inhabitants of gay Naples. It would seem as if the conventual life must have some peculiar charm attaching to it, when we find that wherever no legal obstacles are thrown in the way of monastic establishments, they exist in numbers that would scarcely be credited by most English people, and that they are constantly on the increase.

A third convent which I visited in the environs of Naples, was that of the Alcantarists at Portici, called San Pietro di Alcantara. This was the first House of the Order of Alcantarists I had visited. It is prettily situated on the seashore, near the railway station, its walls being washed by the Bay of Naples, and having a terrace, *a l'Italiano*, immediately overhanging the sea. Before visiting the convent itself, I went into its little church, which was being gaily decorated with coloured hangings, in preparation for some local festival. As I was resting on a bench, a bell tolled for a few minutes, and on its cessation, the friars began the recitation of their

ALCANTARIST CONVENT AT PORTICI. 313

morning Office from within the choir, which as usual in Italian monasteries, is placed behind the high altar, and screened by doors or curtains on either side of the altar from the view of persons in the body of the church. Assembled round the convent gate, as I entered it, were a number of poor people of both sexes, awaiting the distribution of the soup, or other charity, which is served out at noon daily at the gate of most religious houses of the Mendicant Orders.

The Alcantarists are one of the half dozen Orders or more which bear the name, and follow the rule of St. Francis of Assisi. Their habit of snuff-coloured serge so closely resembles that worn by other branches of Franciscans, and especially the Recollects, that I mistook them for the latter. But I had the good fortune to be shewn over the convent by a young and courteous friar, Padre Buonaventura, who set me right on this point, and also gave me some information of interest in regard to his Order. I learnt from him, among other things, that convents of this Order were not numerous except in Naples and in Spain; and that the Alcantarists live exclusively on alms, not being even allowed (like some other Franciscans) to receive foundations for masses; and moreover that they rise to Matins at midnight. Padre Buonaventura also told me that this convent then contained thirty-five friars, and that there was a "studio," or class there for philosophy, for young members of the Order preparing to take priest's orders.

To return from the vicinity of Naples to the city itself, I will mention a few other convents which I went over, from among the numerous religious houses with which Naples abounded. The Convent of St. Antony of Padua, (also called San Lorenzo), was one of these. It has a handsome cloister, where I noticed some curious old Latin epitaphs; and leading out of the cloister is a chapter-house that merits attention. Ascending the staircase from the cloister, I walked through the dormitories, which are spacious, the principal one being of great length. Over each cell door was a painting in fresco of some saint. The friars here were Franciscans, belonging to the Order of Conventuals, called in Italy, "Conventuali." As has been mentioned before in describing other convents of the same Order, the Conventuals wear a black habit, with a very thin white cord round the waist. Unlike Franciscans generally, they are allowed to receive endowments, and are therefore reckoned among the *Possidenti*, or Endowed Orders. The community here was numerous, comprising about sixty friars.

I also visited a small monastery of Carmelites in the Strada Santa Teresa a Chiaja, the street deriving its name from the convent, which is dedicated to St. Teresa, the great Spanish saint, who flourished in the sixteenth century. The friars of this convent belong to St. Teresa's reform of the Carmelites, popularly called, after her, Teresiani, an Order which I have already had occasion to mention. Their habit is brown, like that of the Franciscans, but they wear over it a white cloak, and a white three-cornered clerical hat. The convent is small, but it has a pretty little cloister, where I used sometimes to walk on hot summer mornings, the hotel where I was staying being in the same street. The church also is pretty, and is approached by a handsome double flight of steps. In the church was a large image of the Madonna, splendidly attired, and protected by a glass case of immense size. These richly robed images of the Virgin in glass cases, standing out in a prominent place in the churches, and the objects of popular veneration, are one of the religious characteristics of Southern Italy.

The large Convent of the Gesù Nuovo was another of those that I visited. Its church is one of the finest in Naples, and decorated with frescoes by Lanfranco and Solimene. Among the easel paintings is a picture by Guercino. The entire building is incrusted and paved with marble. The convent belonged to the Jesuits, of whom there was here a numerous community, and whose Order generally was among the most flourishing in the kingdom of Naples. One of the Jesuit fathers, who told me he had been in England, spoke English very fairly. The Convent of San Filippo Neri, the church and cloister of which I visited, belonged to an Order known by the name of the Padri Gerolimini. Its church ranks among the finest in Naples, and merits particular attention from its architecture, its profusion of marble, its paintings, and twelve splendid columns of granite, by which the aisles are separated from the nave.

Naples abounded with convents of nuns of every Order, but these of course I was not able to visit. Among them, I may mention the Convent of Santa Chiara, with its stately church. I remember noticing in the latter a poor woman kneeling before an altar, convulsed in tears, and sobbing loudly, apparently in a paroxysm of grief, which continued throughout my stay in the church. This was quite a Southern demonstration of feeling. I likewise visited the church of another nunnery—a monastery of Franciscans—commonly called "Trentatre," or thirty-three, that being the fixed number of the sisterhood, in memory of the thirty-three years of Christ's life on earth.

I here conclude these notes of my Italian tour in 1857. Within a fortnight after bidding adieu to the busy activity, the gay cheerfulness, the manifold beauties, and the glorious climate of Naples, I was again in England, with feelings akin to those of Catullus, when, on returning after a journey to his favourite retreat on the Lake of Garda, he exclaimed:

"O quid solutis est beatius curis
Cum mens onus reponit, ac peregrino
Labore fessi venimus larem ad nostrum,
Desideratoque acquiescimus lecto?"

CHAPTER XVII.

Miscellaneous Memoranda concerning Italian Monasteries.

In the preceding chapters I have given a continuous narrative of the visits that I made to various monasteries during two successive tours in Italy, in the years 1856 and 1857, commencing with my sojourn at the convent of San Bartolommeo degli Armeni, at Genoa. In addition, however, to the monasteries described in those chapters, I visited a few others at different times, and in the course of other journeys to Italy; and of these I propose to give a brief notice in the present chapter.

The rising sun was gilding the snow-clad peaks of the Mont Cenis, and filling the sky with its purple tints, when, after a moonlight ascent of the pass, I arrived at the summit of what an old Greek author calls τὸ τεῖχος 'Ιταλίας, the wall of Italy—and saw for the first time, the plains of Piedmont spread out before me. This was in the beginning of February, 1856, at which season the whole mountain was covered with snow, so that the ascent and descent of the pass had to be made in sledges. After descending the zigzag road at so rapid a pace as to seem almost dangerous, we arrived in a short time at Susa, the Segusium of the Romans, now an episcopal town of some three or four thousand inhabitants. It is beautifully placed in the midst of lovely scenery, on the banks of the Dora-Susina, from the bridge over which stream a charming view may be obtained. Susa contains a celebrated Roman arch, besides other ancient remains, and also a cathedral well worth visiting. Not the least interesting object, however, that I saw at Susa, was a small Franciscan convent standing almost opposite to the railway station, in strange contrast with the busy animation of the latter.

When I approached the convent, its porch was filled by the lame, the blind, and the halt, eager expectants, apparently, of the convent charity. I rang the bell, and asked the barefooted friar who opened the gate, whether I could be allowed to see the interior. "Non c'è niente à vedere," ("there is nothing to be seen") was his reply. Nevertheless, I repeated my request, and he then said he would admit me after he had finished attending on the poor.

In a few minutes he accordingly took me into the convent, and leading the way to the vine-trellised garden, he left me there.

At the farther end of the garden were five friars pacing to and fro, engaged in conversation, who, as soon as they observed my approach, advanced to meet me, saluting me at the same time very courteously. These were Capuchin Friars, (to which Order the convent belonged), and were all in priest's orders. They wore the usual Franciscan brown habit, together with sandals on their feet, and beards on their chins, the latter practice, as has been previously stated, being peculiar to the Capuchins among the several branches of Franciscans. The friars conducted me over the convent, which to me was very interesting, being almost the first monastery I had ever entered; but after the many larger establishments of the kind already described, it is unnecessary to give a particular description of the several parts of this convent. I was shewn an apartment of considerable size, which was used, as I was told, by the Bishop of Susa, when he came there to make a "spiritual retreat." The convent church, although small and unpretending, is pretty.

From Susa I proceeded by railway to Turin,

the leading characteristic of which city is the geometrical regularity of the streets, which run straight as arrows, and at right angles to one another. In this respect it is strikingly unlike other Italian towns, which are usually as remarkable for their quaint irregular outline, as Turin is for its prim symmetry. Many of its streets and piazzas, however, are very handsome, and it contains several fine churches and other public buildings.

On a commanding eminence beyond the Po, called Il Monte, is situated a large Capuchin convent, which I had been recommended to see by the friars at Susa, and to which I therefore repaired before leaving Turin. It was of great extent, and numbered within its walls no less than eighty friars, but it did not appear to be otherwise remarkable, at least not after the numerous houses of the Order that I have since seen. I heard here, for the first time, of the large mother house of the Capuchin Order at Rome, where I afterwards had the good fortune to pass several months.

In the autumn of 1858, I made a tour in Northern Italy, which I entered on this occasion by the fine pass of the Splügen. After three weeks' boating amid the lovely scenery of

Lake Como,* I had a delightful tour to the Lake of Lugano, and Bellinzona, (the capital of Swiss Italy), and afterwards to the Lago Maggiore, the whole length of which I travelled over by steamboat, stopping, en route, for a few days at Baveno, and the Borromean Islands. Thence I made a second visit to Milan—in which my first impression of the unparalleled magnificence of its splendid Duomo was fully confirmed. From Milan I travelled through the Duchy of Parma, and found much to interest me in its two principal cities, Parma and Piacenza.

Parma is a town of considerable size, and situated on the river of the same name. It has a handsome Piazza Grande, and several good

---

* The cathedral of Como merits, I think, more attention than it usually receives, either from tourists, or from those who have written on Italy and its numberless beauties. This cathedral is a beautiful specimen of Italian Gothic, and bears a resemblance in its general character to the Duomo of Milan, although of course on a very much smaller scale. Besides a handsome Gothic interior, it is so beautiful externally, as to constitute it, in my judgment, one of the finest churches of Italy, in regard at least to its exterior. Like the cathedral of Milan, it is adorned with numerous statues and graceful turrets, and is enriched by several elegant portals in the best style of Renaissance. One of these gateways especially—that on the north side of the cathedral—deserves particular examination.

streets, especially those of San Michele, Sta. Lucia, San Barnaba, and dei Genovesi. The cathedral has a fine Lombard exterior, and the interior also is very beautiful. Its cupola is embellished with exquisite frescoes by Correggio, for whose paintings Parma is famous. The church of San Giovanni, and the Public Gallery, likewise contain some chefs-d'œuvres by the same master. The "Teatro Farnesina," said to be the largest theatre existing, was constructed in the fifteenth century, on the model of an ancient Greek theatre, and formed an object of great interest in connexion with Parma; but it was intended shortly, as I was informed, to pull it down, on account of its bad state of repair.

Piacenza, which formerly constituted a separate duchy of itself, is a large fortified town, and its battlements and towers give it an imposing appearance as you approach it, whether from the side of Milan, or that of Parma. The principal objects of interest are the Cathedral, and the great piazza, which is adorned by two celebrated equestrian statues in bronze, and by a Gothic hotel-de-ville. Piacenza also contains many other churches, among the principal of which, on account of its frescoes, is that of La Madonna della Campagna.

The church of La Madonna della Campagna is conventual, belonging to the adjoining Franciscan convent. The church was originally built by Bramante, but its proportions have been since a good deal altered. The fresco paintings are numerous and very beautiful, especially those by Pordenone, which are worthy of careful study. As I was examining Pordenone's fine frescoes in the cupola of this church, a Franciscan friar passed across the nave towards the convent. I asked him whether I could see the latter, to which he replied by politely conducting me over the whole monastery, which proved large and highly interesting. It was tenanted by the branch of the Franciscan Order called "Riformati," or Recollects, whose brown habit and cord closely resemble those of the Capuchins; but the two are easily distinguishable, from the absence, in the case of the Recollects, of the long beard which forms the leading characteristic in the personal appearance of the Capuchin friars.

Among the other parts of this convent which the friar shewed me, was the spacious refectory, the oak tables of which were laid ready for dinner. On a number of rough earthenware jugs and cups, (the latter being used instead of glasses), placed at regular intervals along the tables, were painted the arms of the Franciscan Order, consisting of a cross with a human arm on either side of it, bearing in the palms of the hands the impress of the Saviour's wounds, known by the name of the "Stigmas of Saint Francis." There were at this period about forty-five friars here. The friar who conducted me over the convent, informed me that Piacenza then contained within its walls some eight or ten religious houses of different Orders.

From Piacenza I travelled, partly by carriage, and partly by railway, to Genoa, over a portion of the course of the ancient Roman road between Piacenza and Genoa, called the Via Posthumia,* passing by two of the Roman stations, viz., Vicus Iriæ, now Voghera, and Dertona, now Tortona. It was a soft autumnal evening, following a beautiful sunset, on which I arrived at Genoa; and as I passed through its narrow, winding, picture-like streets—at the corners of many of which were images of the Madonna,

---

* The Via Posthumia is mentioned in the Bronze Tablet of Genoa, which fixes its date at not less than a century before the Christian era. This Tablet—which is preserved in the "municipio"—is nearly, if not quite, the only relic of classical days in connexion with Genoa that has come down to us.

with little oil lamps burning beneath them—I was much impressed with the combination this fine old city presents of busy prosperity and cheerful gaiety, with the artistic effects and historical associations of a middle-age town.

During a sojourn of about three weeks at Genoa, I visited my monastic friends at San Bartolommeo, and San Barnaba, besides some of my acquaintances in one or two other convents, such as the handsome Oratorian house of San Filippo Neri, and the Carmelite monastery of San Carlo, in the Strada Balbi. I have not before mentioned the Capuchin *ospicio* annexed to the great hospital at Genoa. It contains about twenty friars, whose special duty it is to attend on the sick. They recite the whole office of the Breviary daily in two services only, that they may have more time to devote to the patients. These friars use the chapel of St. Catherine of Genoa, adjoining the hospital, in common, I believe, with the Brignole nuns (also attached to the hospital,) though of course at different hours. Whenever, abroad, you visit a hospital, you will see the quiet, zealous nun actively engaged in her work of charity; and, at least in Italy, you will also see the humble, bare-footed Mendicant friar going from bedside to bedside, administering the consolations of religion to helpless sufferers.

I will conclude my account of Italian convents, with a few words concerning those of Nice; for, well known as this favourite winter residence is to English people, it is probable that its conventual establishments are scarcely known at all, except some of them by name.

I was at Nice in the summer of 1859, when it was almost deserted by the English and other visitors. I arrived there from Provence, having left the railway at Avignon, whence I had an interesting journey by Apt to Digne, in the Basses Alpes. From Digne I travelled by the fine Alpine road to Grasse, joining the ordinary route from Marseilles to Nice at Cannes. I was struck by the peculiarly Italian character of Nice. This character seems to me to be especially illustrated by its architecture, both domestic and ecclesiastical; as well as by the similarity of its trees and fruits to those seen in other parts of Italy. The practice of painting the exterior of the houses, for example, imparts to Nice an appearance far more in common with Genoa, than with a French town; and the thoroughly Italian style of its churches, again, is in marked contrast with the Gothic type prevailing in Provence, and in France generally. So also the productions of nature—such as the orange and lemon, the aloe and cactus, the graceful palm, and the large-sized olive trees, in place of the small trees of the kind in the south of France—tell of the land "wo die Citronen blühen,"* rather than of the neighbouring country to which it has now become politically annexed. Nor is the language French, except as the medium of intercourse between the foreign visitors and the Nizzois, the dialect known as the Nizzard being the ordinary language of the people.

The conventual establishments likewise remind one of Italy, not only by their number, but also by the large size and antiquity of the monasteries themselves. The principal religious houses in Nice and its vicinity, are a Convent of Recollects, one of Capuchins, two of Oblats of St. Mary, one of Christian Brothers, one of Carmelites, on the road towards Monaco, and about four convents of nuns. Of these, I shall select three of the most important—Cimiers, St. Barthélemy, and St. Pons—for special notice.

* "Kennst du das Land wo die Citronen blühen?"
Goethe.

Nice is built on the banks of the Paglione, a mountain torrent dividing the town into two unequal parts, the larger and older part being on the eastern side of the stream. On the western side of the Puglione, and at the northern extremity of Nice, stands, on a commanding eminence, the large Franciscan monastery of Cimiers, well known, at least externally, to all visitors to Nice. Cimiers, (originally the site of a Roman town called " Civitas Cemeliensis") also gives name to a sort of suburb of Nice, which is a favourite residence of the foreign visitors. I was shewn over every part of this interesting convent by one of the friars, Padre F——, including two pretty little cloisters, the refectory, the dormitories, the cells, the gardens, the church, and the convent cemetery. The friars here are Recollects. I remember, on the first occasion of my visiting Cimiers, six years previously, that I inquired whether these friars were not Capuchins, having been given to understand that such was the case. My informant, a lay-brother, replied, "Non, les Capuchins ont la barbe," at the same time suiting the action to the word, by raising his clenched hand to his chin, in illustration of his meaning. On my asking the same brother if the Franciscan rule was not arduous to follow, he answered with a placid calmness that had characterised his manner throughout, "Il faut avoir de la patience."

The church, the front of which was restored in a Gothic style some fifteen years ago, contains a good painting by Ludovico Brea, a native of Nice. The little convent cemetery is particularly pretty, and is adorned by several handsome monuments. Not the least interesting part of this monastery are its extensive gardens, and the fine view which, owing to their great elevation, may be obtained from them. Padre F—— informed me that the number of friars was then twenty-five, of whom sixteen were in priest's orders, and nine lay-brothers.

The Capuchin convent of St. Barthélemy, within an easy walk of Nice, is a large and picturesque old monastery. It stands in a lovely situation amid hills covered to the top with olive trees, and commands a beautiful view over Nice and the Mediterranean. The cloister, forming a quadrangle as usual, is decorated, according to the Capuchin practice, with numerous rough woodcuts of saints of the Order, under which is printed an epitome of their lives. The dormitories of this convent are exceedingly pretty, and have a thoroughly monastic appearance, as indeed has the whole convent, together with its Franciscan inmates, of whom there were at that time seventeen, viz., ten priests, and seven lay-brothers.

I arrived about mid-day, just as the convent bell was sounding the Ave Maria. At the same time several of the friars—with their long beards, brown habit, sandalled feet, and corded waists— were walking at leisure up and down the cloister, conversing with one another, this being their hour of recreation. I was shewn the convent by Fra Giovanni da Cloanzo, who told me that it was founded in 1555 by the Benedictines of St. Pons, who used to receive annually from the friars of St. Barthélemy, a pail of water in token of their dependence on the abbey. There is a large garden belonging to the convent, from which I took a slight sketch of it. Fra Giovanni afterwards served some dinner for me, *al cappucino*, in the refectory.

I had scarcely finished my frugal meal, when the convent bell began to ring for vespers. This was at two o'clock. I went into the choir to hear the brotherhood perform their office, which they recited with much solemnity of manner. When vespers were ended, I spoke for a few minutes with the Guardian in the cloister. He told me, among other things, that he had been only three weeks before at San Barnaba, near Genoa, where I had stayed two years previously, and where, he added in reply to a question from me, everything was going on prosperously. I was much pleased with my visit to St. Barthélemy, which appeared to be in a flourishing state.

The handsome convent of St. Pons is well situated on the western bank of the Paglione, in the same direction as Cimiers, but at a lower elevation than it. The full-sized windows and spacious chambers of St. Pons, tell of its having been built for an Endowed Order like the Benedictines, to whom, prior to the French Revolution, it belonged—contrasting in this respect with the rows of tiny windows and diminutive cells of the two convents of Mendicants last described. St. Pons is now tenanted by Oblats of St. Mary, the community consisting of twenty-two priests, and ten lay-brothers. They wear a black habit, and their Superior has the title of " Padre Rettore." The Order is an active one, its special functions being to instruct divinity students "nel morale," and to preach in parish churches. It is a new Order, having been instituted, I believe, only about thirty-five or forty years ago.

I entered the convent soon after the dinner hour of the brotherhood, when they were in recreation. Several of the Padri were standing in the handsome cloister around one of their number, who was seated in the midst of them, and reading aloud from a newspaper, in which all appeared much interested. Others were in the open space enclosed by the cloister, playing at a game with wooden balls, which has been already mentioned as a favourite pastime among the religious Orders. One of the community, Padre O——, told me that St. Pons was martyred here in the early ages of Christianity, and that this monastery was founded by St. Siagrus, (or some such name), who, according to my informant, was a nephew of Charlemagne. The convent church is small, and does not present any point of particular interest, except a few paintings of the time of its former Benedictine tenants.

This was the last of more than threescore Italian monasteries that I visited, forming, however, only a mere fraction of the conventual establishments scattered over the length and breadth of Italy; a country which, besides its other characteristics—such as being, *par excellence*, the land of classical associations, and the fine arts, of song and of imagination——is also pre-eminently the land of convents, with the varied associations, mediæval, artistic, and poetical, connected with the name.

> "And now farewell to ITALY—perhaps
> For ever! Yet, methinks, I could not go,
> I could not leave it, were it mine to say,
> Farewell for ever!"

> "But now a long farewell! Oft, while I live,
> If once again in England, once again
> In my own chimney nook, as Night steals on,
> With half-shut eyes reclining, oft, methinks,
> While the wind blusters and the drenching rain
> Clatters without, shall I recall to mind
> The scenes, occurrences, I met with here
> And wander in Elysium; many a note
> Of wildest melody, magician-like
> Awakening, such as the CALABRIAN horn
> Along the mountain-side, when all is still,
> Pours forth at folding-time; and many a chant,
> Solemn, sublime, such as at midnight flows
> From the full choir, when richest harmonies
> Break the deep silence of thy glens, LA CAVA;
> To him who lingers there with listening ear
> Now lost and now descending as from Heaven!"*

* Rogers.

APPENDIX.

LORD MACAULAY, AND LAURENCE STERNE ON BEGGING FRIARS.

The following striking passages from writers of eminence, bearing as they do directly on the subject of the present volume, are well worthy of quotation. In the first extract, Lord Macaulay, with his usual pointedness of expression, states his view of the Philosophy of the institution of the Mendicant Orders. In the second, Sterne draws a life-like portrait, not unmixed with pathos, of the begging friar of the last century.

FROM LORD MACAULAY'S ESSAY ON—"RANKE'S 'HISTORY OF THE POPES.'"

"If we went at large into this most interesting subject we should fill volumes. We will, therefore, at present, advert to only one important part of the policy of the Church of Rome. She thoroughly understands, what no other Church has ever understood, how to deal with enthusiasts. In some sects, particularly in infant sects, enthusiasm is suffered to be rampant. In other sects, particularly in sects long established and richly endowed, it is regarded with aversion. The Catholic Church neither submits to enthusiasm nor proscribes it, but uses it." * She knows that, when religious feelings have obtained the complete empire of the mind, they impart a strange energy, that they raise men above the dominion of pain and pleasure, that obloquy becomes glory, that death itself is contemplated only as the beginning of a higher and happier life. She knows that a person in this state is no object of contempt.* * She accordingly enlists him in her service, assigns to him some forlorn hope, in which intrepidity and impetuosity are more wanted than judgment and self-command, and sends him forth with her benedictions and her applause.

"In England, it not unfrequently happens that a tinker or coalheaver hears a sermon, or falls in with a tract which alarms him about the state of his soul. If he be a man of excitable nerves and strong imagination, he thinks himself given over to the evil power. He doubts whether he has not committed the unpardonable sin. He imputes every wild fancy that springs up in his mind to the whisper of a fiend. His sleep is broken by dreams of the great judgment-seat, the open books, and the unquenchable fire. If in order to escape from these vexing thoughts, he flies to amusement, or to licentious indulgence, the delusive relief only makes his misery darker and more hopeless. At length a turn takes place. He is reconciled to his offended Maker. To borrow the fine imagery of one who had himself been thus tried, he emerged from the Valley of the Shadow of Death, from the dark land of gins and snares, of quagmires and precipices, of evil spirits and ravenous beasts. The sunshine is on his path. He ascends the Delectable Mountains, and catches from their summit a distant view of the shining city which is the end of his pilgrimage. Then arises in his mind a natural and surely not a censurable desire, to impart to others the thoughts of which his own heart is full, to warn the careless, to comfort those who are troubled in spirit." " For a man thus minded, there is within the pale of the establishment no place. He has been at no college; he cannot construe a Greek author or write a Latin theme; and he is told that, if he remains in the communion of the Church, he must do so as a hearer, and that, if he is resolved to be a teacher, he must begin by being a schismatic. His choice is soon made. He harangues on Tower Hill or in Smithfield. A congregation is formed. A license is obtained. A plain brick building, with a desk and benches, is run up, and named Ebenezer or Bethel. In a few weeks the Church has lost for ever a hundred families, not one of which entertained the least scruple about her articles, her liturgy, her government, or her ceremonies.

"Far different is the policy of Rome. The ignorant enthusiast whom the Anglican Church makes an enemy, and, whatever the polite and learned may think, a most dangerous enemy, the Catholic Church makes a champion. She bids him nurse his beard, covers him with a gown and hood of coarse dark stuff, ties a rope round his waist, and sends him forth to teach in her name. He costs her nothing. He takes not a ducat away from the revenues of her beneficed clergy. He lives by the alms of those who respect his spiritual character, and are grateful for his instructions. He preaches, not exactly in the style of Massillon, but in a way which moves the passions of uneducated hearers; and all his influence is employed to strengthen the Church of which he is a minister. To that Church he becomes as strongly attached as any of the cardinals whose scarlet carriages and liveries crowd the entrance of the palace on the Quirinal. In this way the Church of Rome unites in herself all the strength of establishment, and all the strength of dissent. With the utmost pomp of a dominant hierarchy above, she has all the energy of the voluntary system below. It would be easy to mention very recent instances in which the hearts of hundreds of thousands, estranged from her by the selfishness, sloth, and cowardice of the beneficed clergy, have been brought back by the zeal of the begging friars."

FROM STERNE'S "SENTIMENTAL JOURNEY."

THE MONK.

"I had scarce uttered the words when a poor monk, of the order of St. Francis, came into the room, to beg something for his convent.* * * The moment I cast my eyes upon him I was predetermined not to give him a single sous; and accordingly I put my purse into my pocket, buttoned it up, set myself a little more on my centre, and advanced up gravely to him. There was something, I fear, forbidding in my look. I have his figure this moment before my eyes, and think there was that in it which deserved better.

"The monk, as I judge from the break in his tonsure (a few scattered white hairs upon his temples being all that remained of it) might be about seventy; but from his eyes, and that sort of fire which was in them, which seemed more tempered by courtesy than years, could be no more than sixty—truth might lie between—he was certainly sixty-five; and the general air of his countenance, notwithstanding something seemed to have been planting wrinkles in it before their time, agreed to the account.

"It was one of those heads which Guido has often painted—mild, pale, penetrating; free from all common-place ideas of fat, contented ignorance looking downwards upon the earth—it looked forwards; but looked as if it looked at something beyond this world. How one of his order came by it, heaven above, who let it fall upon a monk's shoulders, best knows; but it would have suited a Brahmin, and had I met it upon the plains of Indostan, I had revereuced it.

"The rest of his outline may be given in a few strokes; one might put it into the hands of any one to design, for it was neither elegant nor otherwise, but as character and expression made it so; it was a thin, spare form, something above the common size, if it lost not the distinction by a bend forwards in the figure—but it was the attitude of Entreaty; and as it now stands presented to my imagination, it gained more than it lost by it.

"When he had entered the room three paces, he stood still; and laying his left hand upon his breast (a slender white staff, with which he journeyed, being in his right)—when I had got close up to him, he introduced himself with a little story of the wants of his convent, and the poverty of his order—and did it with so simple a grace—and such an air of deprecation was there in the whole cast of his look and figure—I was bewitched not to have been struck with it. A better reason was, I had predetermined not to give him a single sous.

"'T is very true, said I, replying to a cast upward with his eyes, with which he had concluded his address—'t is very true—and heaven be their resource who have no other but the charity of the world, the stock of which, I fear, is no

APPENDIX. 339

way sufficient for the many *great claims* which are hourly made upon it.

As I pronounced the words *great claims*, he gave a slight glance with his eye downwards upon the sleeve of his tunic. I felt the full force of the appeal: I acknowledge it, said I —a coarse habit (and that but once in three years), with meagre diet, are no great matters; and the true point of pity is, as they can be earned in the world with so little industry, that your order should wish to procure them by pressing upon a fund which is the property of the lame, the blind, the aged, and the infirm; the captive who lies down counting over and over again the days of his affliction, languishes also for his share of it; and had you been of the *order of mercy*, instead of the order of St. Francis, poor as I am, continued I, pointing at my portmanteau, full cheerfully should it have been opened to you for the ransom of the unfortunate. The monk made me a bow. But of all others, returned I, the unfortunate of our own country, surely, have the first rights; and I have left thousands in distress upon our own shore. The monk gave a cordial wave with his head, as much as to say, no doubt, there is misery enough in every corner of the world, as well as within our convent. But we distinguish, said I, laying my hand upon the sleeve of his tunic, in return for his appeal, we distinguish, my good father, betwixt those who wish only to eat the bread of their own labour, and those who eat the bread of other people, and have no other plan in life but to get through it in sloth and ignorance, *for the love of God.*

The poor Franciscan made no reply—a hectic of a moment passed across his cheek, but could not tarry—Nature seemed to have done with her resentments in him; he showed none—but letting his staff fall within his arm, he pressed both his hands with resignation upon his breast, and retired.

My heart smote me the moment he shut the door. " Psha !" said I, with an air of carelessness, three several times—but it would not do: every ungracious syllable I had uttered crowded back into my imagination: I reflected I had no

z 2

right over the poor Franciscan but to deny him; and that the punishment of that was enough to the disappointed without the addition of unkind language. I considered his grey hairs; his courteous figure seemed to re-enter, and gently ask me what injury he had done me, and why I could use him thus? I would have given twenty livres for an advocate. I have behaved very ill, said I within myself; but I have only just set out upon my travels, and shall learn better manners as I get along."

II.

LIST OF ITALIAN MONASTERIES VISITED BY THE AUTHOR.

Benedictine Abbey of San Paolo fuori delle mura near Rome.
Benedictine Abbey of San Domenico at Sienna.
Cistercian Abbey of Santa Croce in Gerusalemme at Rome.
Cistercian Abbey of San Bernardo at Rome.
Abbey of La Coronata (Regular Canons of St. Austin) near Genoa.
Abbey of San Teodoro (Regular Canons of St. Austin) at Genoa.
Abbey of San Gregorio sul monte Celio (Camaldolesi monks) at Rome.
Carthusian Priory of Sta. Maria degli Angeli at Rome.
Carthusian Priory of La B. Vergine delle Grazie, near Pavia.
Carthusian Priory of San Martino at Naples.
Dominican Priory of Sta Sabina at Rome.
Dominican Priory at Bologna.
Dominican Priory of San Marco at Florence.
Dominican Priory of Il Castello at Genoa.
Carmelite Priory of Sta. Maria Transteverina at Rome.
Carmelite Priory of La Madonna della Vittoria at Rome.
Carmelite Priory of San Martino in Monte at Rome.
Carmelite Priory of San Carlo at Genoa.

Carmelite Priory of Sta. Anna at Genoa.
Carmelite Priory of Sta. Teresa a Chiaja at Naples.
Convent of St. Antony of Padua (Conventuals) at Padua.
Convent of San Francesco d'Albaro (Conventuals) near Genoa.
Convent of St. Antony of Padua (Conventuals) at Naples.
Observant Convent of Sta. Maria in Ara Cœli at Rome.
Observant Convent of Sant' Isidoro at Rome.
Observant Convent of La Annunziata at Genoa.
Observant Convent of Oregina near Genoa.
Capuchin Convent of La Madonna della Concezione at Rome.
Capuchin Convent of San Lorenzo fuori delle mura near Rome.
Capuchin Convent at Albano.
Capuchin Convent at Velletri.
Capuchin Convent at Genzano.
Capuchin Convent at Frascati.
Capuchin Convent of La Madonna della Concezione at Genoa.
Capuchin Hospice (or Convent) adjoining the Hospital at Genoa.
Capuchin Convent of San Barnaba near Genoa.
Capuchin Convent of Campi near Genoa.
Capuchin Convent of San Martino at Sestri Ponente.
Capuchin Convent of San Nicola near Voltri.
Capuchin Convent at Varazze.
Capuchin Convent at Savona.
Capuchin Convent of Sta. Maria degli Angeli at Quiliano.
Capuchin Convent at Turin.
Capuchin Convent at Susa.
Capuchin Convent of St. Barthélemy near Nice.
Convent of Il Monte (Recollects) near Genoa.
Convent of La Madonna della Campagna (Recollects) at Piacenza.
Convent of Cimiers (Recollects) at Nice.
Alcantarist Convent at Portici.
Convent of Camaldolesi Hermits near Naples.

Convent of Minims at Genoa.

Convent of La Trinità (Trinitarians) in the Via Condotti at Rome.

Passionist Convent at Rome.

Barnabite Convent of San Carlo ai Catenari at Rome.

Barnabite Convent of San Bartolommeo degli Armeni at Genoa.

Jesuit Convent of Il Gesù Nuovo at Naples.

Convent of the Padri Crociferi at Genoa.

Convent of the Padri Scolopi at Genoa.

Lazarist Convent at Genoa.

Convent of St. Pons (Oblats of St. Mary) at Nice.

Oratorian Convent of San Filippo Neri at Genoa.

Convent of I Sacri Cuori in Transtevere at Rome.

Convent of the Sacré Cœur at La Trinità dei Monti at Rome.

NOTES.

A

Since a large part of this volume was in type, several recently published statistical tables of the Monastic Orders have come under my notice, the substance of which I transcribe, as they can hardly fail, I think, to prove interesting to the reader.

According to one of these tables, it appears that there were in Rome, in June, 1861, 1,385 secular priests, (exclusive of 40 bishops), 2,474 monks, and 2,032 nuns. These figures (and I believe them to be authentic) do not bear out the statement of a recent traveller in Italy—which is accompanied by some rather severe strictures on the alleged fact—that there are in Rome, 10,000 priests, "mostly in the prime of life," (Dicey's "Rome in 1860"). The 2,474 monks include doubtless the lay-brothers, who constitute probably a third of the whole, which leaves about 1,650 monks in holy orders. These, added to the 1,385 secular priests, and 40 bishops, would make the number of persons in priest's orders at Rome 3,075, instead of 10,000; and even if no deduction be made for the lay-brothers in the religious communities, the number would still be under 4,000.

There are, it appears, at present in the world, 7,231 members of the Society of Jesus, or Jesuits, of whom 1,035 are Italians, 2,203 French, 912 Austrians and Germans, 642 Belgians, 206 Dutch, 136 Gallicians, 740 Spaniards and Portuguese, 265 English, 126 Irish, 240 North Americans, and 220 belonging to other States of America. The number of Jesuits present at Rome in June last, was 289. The Order has three provinces in France—that of Paris containing 1,053 members; that of Lyons, 626; and that of Toulouse, 524. According to the same table, the Jesuits in Italy are subdivided as follows. The province of Rome comprises 462 members;

that of Turin, 277; Venetia contains 226; Naples, 463; and Sicily, 207. Of those whose convents have been suppressed in Italy, many have been sent to Germany, Belgium, England, and America.

A statistical table has been lately published at Naples, purporting to give the statistics of the conventual establishments in the Neapolitan provinces on the 17th of February 1901. According to this table, there were then 1,020 convents of men, containing 13,611 monks, of whom 3,055 belonged to the Endowed Orders, with an annual revenue of 3,323,795 francs. Of these 3,055, 1924 were in holy orders, and 1,131 lay-brothers. There were also 1,657 Mendicant Friars, possessing a revenue of 1,232,182 frs.; and 8,899 absolute Mendicants without revenues. Of these last, 5,352 were in holy orders, and 3,517 lay-brothers.*

The number of nunneries is stated to have been 276, containing 8,001 nuns, (viz., 6,103 choir sisters, and 2,898 novices and lay-sisters), with a yearly revenue of 4,772,704 francs. The statement from which these figures are taken seems to take no account of the convents of Mendicant nuns, the endowed nunneries only being apparently enumerated.

B

I will here add a few words to the account that has been already given of conventual diet. (See Chapters, I, V, and X). In the first place it should be borne in mind that members of religious communities in Italy rise at a very early hour, (five or six o'clock), and take nothing but a single cup of coffee without milk, and a mouthful or two of dry bread, until about mid-day, when they dine. In the Mendicant Orders, not only are the portions of each friar very limited in quantity, but the quality also is generally coarse, and often far from nutritious. Thus, although on days which are not fasts, meat is usually allowed, I do not think, (writing from memory), that each person's portion exceeds a couple of ounces, and that, too, not of rich juicy meat as in England,

* Several of the Neapolitan monasteries, it would appear, had not sent in their returns when this table was published.

but tough, hard meat, from which whatever goodness it once had has frequently been well nigh boiled away. In these Orders the soup at dinner is the really substantial dish, for besides the scanty portion of indifferent meat, the only other dish is generally either a piece of dried and salted fish, swimming in oil, (" baccalà," in Italian), or else some boiled cabbage or other green vegetable. After this slender meal they have to wait for supper until sunset, which in summer may be eight or nine hours. This meal is still more slender than their dinner. A tiny piece of meat, it is true, is again served out, but this, together with some green vegetable, constitutes the whole repast. As stated in the body of this work, an ample portion of bread is allowed. Their beverage consists of weak wine of the country ready mixed with water. This forms their diet on ordinary days, but on fast days it is yet more spare.

In most of the Endowed Orders a somewhat more liberal dietary prevails in regard to quantity, and still more so in the quality of the provisions and in the style of cooking; but, nevertheless, the diet even of these richer Orders would probably be found wholly insufficient by English gentlemen of the most abstemious habits.

C

I regret that I had not the advantage of reading Mr. Ruskin's " Seven Lamps of Architecture," until the whole of this volume was written, and the greater part of it in print. From his instructive remarks on the Cathedral of Pisa, I apprehend that I have fallen into an error in citing (in Chapter IV) that splendid edifice as an instance in support of my proposition, that most Italian churches possessing fine exteriors are built in a style of architecture foreign to the styles more peculiarly Italian. There seems, indeed, to be some difficulty in assigning any one definite style to the Cathedral of Pisa. Mrs. Starke, in her " Travels in Italy," calls it Greco-Arabian, while Mrs. Jameson (" Diary of an Ennuyée," third edition, page 306) professes herself unable to determine its style, owing to the admixture it exhibits of several different orders of architecture; and I confess that I shared in her uncertainty when I saw this famous church. Mr. Ruskin, however—with apparently good reason—calls it Lombard, and if this be so, it cannot fairly be cited in support of the proposition in question.

While referring to Mr. Ruskin's "Lamps of Architecture," I will quote in confirmation of my observations on the cloister of St. John Lateran, (Chapter IV) the following passage from that work. "It should be observed, that any pattern which gives opponent lines in its parts, may be arranged on lines parallel with the main structure. Thus, rows of diamonds, like spots on a snake's back, or the bones on a sturgeon, are exquisitely applied both to vertical and spiral columns. The loveliest instances of such decoration that I know, are the pillars of the cloister of St. John Lateran, lately illustrated by Mr. Digby Wyatt, in his most valuable and faithful work on antique mosaic." I cannot, however, take leave of this book of Mr. Ruskin's, without expressing my dissent from the terms of strong condemnation in which he speaks of the Leaning Tower of Pisa. Notwithstanding the epithet of "ugly" with which he stigmatises it, (quite irrespective of its inclination) I must still venture to think it a most charming bit of architecture.

D

In Chapter VII it has been stated, perhaps too generally, that the Cistercian lay-brothers wear a brown habit. This is certainly the case with the Reformed Cistercians, or Trappists; but, if I remember rightly, the lay-brothers of Sta. Croce in Gerusalemme, and San Bernardo, at Rome, wear a white habit, like the Padri. This, however, is a point on which, not having taken a note of it at the time, I write only from memory.

E

The reader who has followed the account that has been given in the preceding pages, of the life and manners of the monastic Orders at the present day, will find some interesting references to those Orders—and especially to the begging friars—as they appeared to a discriminating observer of the

13th century, in the letters of Robert Grosseteste, Bishop of Lincoln, temp. Henry III., recently edited by Mr. Luard, (*Roberti Grosseteste Episcopi quondam Lincolniensis Epistola*. Edited by Henry Richards Luard, M.A., Fellow and Assistant Tutor of Trinity College, Cambridge).

Bishop Grosseteste—the famous scholar, who, we are told by Roger Bacon, "alone knew the sciences"—held the Mendicant friars in much esteem; and several characteristic anecdotes are related of him by Mr. Luard, in connexion with these friars. For example, "he once told a preaching friar that three things were necessary for temporal health—food, sleep, and good humour, (*jocus*). To another friar, troubled with melancholy, he enjoined as a penance to drink a cup full of the best wine; and, when it had been drunk very unwillingly, he said to him, 'dearest brother, if you frequently had such a penance, you would have a much better regulated conscience.'" Bishop Grosseteste, as already mentioned, held the Franciscan friars in great respect, and is said to have been particularly pleased to see their dresses patched, as a sign of their poverty. These patches in the coarse serge habit of the Mendicant friars—which several great painters have delighted to copy—have often been noticed by the writer in the course of his travels in Italy. They are especially apparent in the chocolate-coloured dress worn by the Franciscans, the new cloth, of which the patches are made, contrasting with the older portion of the garment, to which time has imparted a lighter tint.

THE END.

LONDON:
Printed by A. Schulze, 13, Poland Street.

Passionist p. 149.

F. G. TRAFFORD'S WORKS.

New and Cheaper Edition, in Crown 8vo. price 5s. bound.

TOO MUCH ALONE.

BY F. G. TRAFFORD,

AUTHOR OF "CITY AND SUBURB."

"We can cordially recommend 'Too Much Alone' to any reader in quest of a thoroughly good novel. It is a well-conceived, well-wrought out story; but we regard it less as a present success than the commencement of a successful career."—ATHENÆUM.

"'Too Much Alone' is an exceedingly suggestive phrase, and what it portends is admirably realised in the novel of which it is the title. It is a thoroughly good novel, both in conception and execution, and ought at once to secure for its Author an honourable popularity. Among the rare combination of qualities which distinguish it, is its downright reality which yet does not preclude an infusion of ideal grace into a story of domestic life."—SPECTATOR.

New and Cheaper Edition, in Crown 8vo. price 6s. bound,

CITY AND SUBURB.

BY F. G. TRAFFORD.

AUTHOR OF "TOO MUCH ALONE."

"This is a first-class work, and cannot fail to attract universal attention. It is one of the most interesting and instructive novels we have ever read."—LONDON REVIEW.

"In pathos, sentiment and vigour the author is almost equally at home, and we do not hesitate to say that he will be carried to a high status amongst the romance writers of the day."—PRESS.

"Sustains the author's right to hold a very high position among contemporary novelists."—SPECTATOR.

"We feel assured that the author is destined to hold a high place in the ranks of English novelists."—LITERARY GAZETTE.

"Will repay perusal with interest. . . . . Decidedly interesting."—ATHENÆUM.

"Opens with great effect. Ruby reminds us of Thackeray's most successful female character—Tiz."—GLOBE.

"Ruby the beauty will stand out as a distinct personage on the reader's memory when the dramatis personæ of half-a-dozen intervening novels have melted into chaos."—SATURDAY REVIEW.

"Has more than common interest attached to it."—OBSERVER.

"We can unhesitatingly recommend the novel to all dwellers in 'City and Suburb.'"—CRITIC.

"The author has given us a really pleasing novel. The story is replete with interest."—MORNING CHRONICLE.

"The announcement of a new work from this author's pen cannot fail to excite curiosity, and arouse expectation of that which is so dear to a novel reader, a really genuine, good novel. In the present instance that expectation is fulfilled; 'City and Suburb' is more than equal in ability and finish to the author's preceding works."—MORNING POST.

CHARLES J. SKEET, PUBLISHER,
10, KING WILLIAM STREET, CHARING CROSS.

ANNOUNCEMENTS.

NEW NOVEL BY F. G. TRAFFORD.

THE WORLD IN THE CHURCH. A Novel, 3 vols. By F. G. TRAFFORD. Author of "Too Much Alone," "City and Suburb," &c.

CONVENT LIFE IN ITALY. By ALGERNON TAYLOR. 1 vol. post 8vo. 10s. 6d.

DANIEL MANIN AND VENICE in 1848-9. By HENRI MARTIN, Author of "L'Histoire de France;" with an Introduction and a Chapter on English Diplomacy relating to Venice, by ISAAC BUTT, Q.C., M.P., Author of "The History of Italy." 2 vols. 21s.

NEW NOVEL BY CAPTAIN WRAXALL.

MARRIED IN HASTE. A Novel, 3 vols. By Captain LASCELLES WRAXALL. Author of "Only a Woman," &c.

CHARLES J. SKEET, PUBLISHER,
10, KING WILLIAM STREET, CHARING CROSS.

www.ingramcontent.com/pod-product-compliance
Lightning Source LLC
Chambersburg PA
CBHW020322240426
43673CB00039B/888